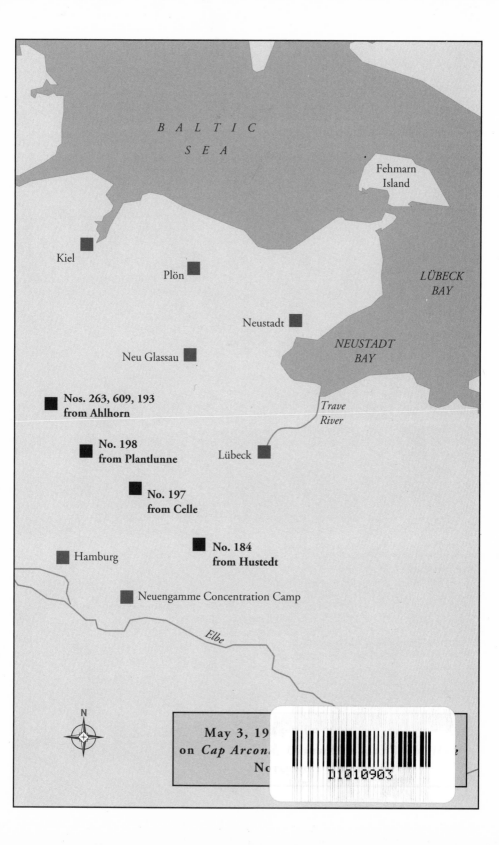

BALTIC
SEA

Fehmarn
Island

Kiel

Plön

*LÜBECK
BAY*

Neustadt

*NEUSTADT
BAY*

Neu Glassau

**Nos. 263, 609, 193
from Ahlhorn**

*Trave
River*

**No. 198
from Plantlunne**

Lübeck

**No. 197
from Celle**

Hamburg

**No. 184
from Hustedt**

Neuengamme Concentration Camp

Elbe

N

**May 3, 19
on *Cap Arcon**
N

THE 100-YEAR SECRET

THE 100-YEAR SECRET

BRITAIN'S HIDDEN WWII MASSACRE

■ ■ ■

Benjamin Jacobs
with Eugene Pool

The Lyons Press
Guilford, Connecticut
An imprint of The Globe Pequot Press

The Lyons Press is an imprint of The Globe Pequot Press.

10 9 8 7 6 5 4 3 2 1

Printed in the United States of America

ISBN 1-59228-532-5

Library of Congress Cataloging-in-Publication Data is available
on file.

*This book is dedicated to the victims
of the disaster in Neustadt Bay.*

TABLE OF CONTENTS

ACKNOWLEDGMENTS

Else Jacobs:

In the name of my husband, Ben Jacobs, who died on January 30, 2004, I would like to thank Eugene Pool for his diligence and dedication in bringing this book to fruition. Sincerest gratitude to our dear friend Jerry Preston for his advice and negotiations in helping to get this book published. Many thanks to a wonderful agent, Fifi Oscard, for her patience and help in finding a publisher. Last but not least, thanks to everyone else (too many names to mention) who helped make this book possible.

Eugene Pool:

First and foremost I would like to thank Benjamin Jacobs for inviting me to help him tell this important story. It was truly an honor to be involved. I also thank Else Jacobs for providing essential first-hand information and unique insights into the incident, as well as unflagging support for the writing of the book. In London, Roger E. Nixon discovered and interpreted British war records that shed significant new light on formerly obscure events. Victor Henningsen provided an extremely helpful close reading of the manuscript. John Foster Leich, who served in Northwest Germany as an American naval liaison to British forces, supplied valuable information on the last days of the war. Attorney William Strong was an important facilitator of the project. Helpful contributions came from Lawrence Bond, James Der-John, Ellen Feld, Dianne Haley, Sally Murphy, Daniel Pool, Robert Porter, Helen Schultz, Robert Shepard, Alice Stern, and students in the Winsor School Autobiography class of 2004 (Caroline Baker, Brianna Connolly, Georgina Coolidge, Julie de Neufville, Erin Gallery, Anuja Khettry, Meg Kiley, Whitney Kufe, Kirstin Mattson-DiCecca, Le-Uyen Tran, Nancy Walton, Meg Weeks, Jessica Wilson, Patricia Zelee, and Maria Zervos). Fifi Oscard was every writer's dream—a literary agent of the highest caliber who found a wonderful publisher in scarcely any time at all. Lyons Press Senior Editor Tom McCarthy made the final shaping of the manuscript a pleasure, rather than a chore. Copyeditor Melissa Hayes reworded awkward phrases as well as caught numerous errors. My son, Nathan, my daughter, Miranda, and my daughter-in-law, Denise, provided important understanding and support. To my wife, Parrish Dobson, I owe my greatest debt—especially for wise words at key moments, not only in this manuscript, but also in my life.

Prologue:
No One Tells This Story

As a light rain began to fall on the afternoon of May 3, 1945, British soldiers of 6 Commando, 1st Special Services Brigade, searched the beaches of Neustadt, Germany on the Baltic Sea for survivors. The bodies of men, women, and even small children lay by the hundreds on the sands. Offshore, under a gray, smoke-scoured sky, the soldiers could see the still-smoldering hulk of the former luxury liner, the *Cap Arcona*, and scores of other damaged ships. A highly effective RAF bombing and rocketing raid had destroyed the fleet and killed over 7,000 concentration camp inmates who had been imprisoned on the ships.

One soldier found a girl of about seven clutching the hand of a woman beside her. He presumed she was the girl's mother. Both bodies were clad in the black-and-white-striped wool garments of concentration camp prisoners. The heads and shoulders of floating corpses were visible just offshore, as victims of all ages drifted in. Even a full year later, the bodies would still be washing up.

Six Commando had arrived with the British 11th Armored Division just an hour earlier, interrupting SS troops, marines, and cadets from Neustadt's U-boat school who were gathered on the shore shooting those survivors of the attack who had somehow managed to swim ashore in the 46-degree Fahrenheit water. The Germans knew the British were coming. They also knew the war in Europe was over. They surrendered immediately, without resistance.

Captain A. D. Pratt put his captives to work hauling and sorting the corpses they had helped produce. Some Hitler Youth and townspeople had come down to join in the shooting, and he ordered them to help with the dead, as well.

I learned all this later. At the time I, myself—Benjamin Jacobs, twenty-five years old, born Berek Jakubowicz in the village of Dobra, Poland—was a mile and a half offshore, treading water, fighting to stay afloat near the flaming wreck of the *Cap Arcona*. I was a concentration camp inmate who had been imprisoned on the ship. With a combination of luck and determination, my older brother Josek and I had managed to escape from a storeroom below decks in which SS troops had locked us and a hundred or so others. Then I had leapt from the burning wreck, leaving my brother behind. He could not swim. Just a few hundred yards away, the freighter *Thielbek*, carrying 2,800 prisoners, was also in flames. Black smoke poured into the sky. The air was filled with the snapping and crackling of towers of flames, as well as the screams of people burning and the cries of the poor souls who had jumped into the icy water.

As a maritime disaster, in terms of lives lost the incident compares only with the sinking of the SS *Wilhelm Gustloff*, torpedoed by a Soviet submarine on January 30, just three months earlier. Close to 8,000 German refugees and wounded soldiers perished that night. While the sinking of the *Titanic* is perhaps the most familiar maritime tragedy, far fewer people—1,543—lost their lives in that event.

Why has a tragedy of such proportions been allowed to disappear from historic memory? How did our supposed allies—the British—become our murderers? Why, in the first place, did the Nazis load us onto these ships in the closing hours of the European war? These questions beg for answers, especially since so few people around the world know of this horrific incident. Unbelievably, it appears in no history books—not in Germany, Great Britain, or the United States. As Lawrence Bond said in his History Channel film, *Typhoons' Last Storm*, the Neustadt Bay incident remains "one of the great tragedies, and one of the least known" of World War II.

No one tells this story—so I must. Otherwise, as memories fade, the tragedy will slowly be forgotten. Out of the more than 7,500 inmates loaded onto the *Cap Arcona* and *Thielbek*, only 350 of us survived.

In the spring of 1945, the SS were evacuating concentration camps all over Germany in a desperate attempt to hide their prisoners from the Allied armies advancing on both fronts. Marshal Zhukov's Red Army was attacking through East Prussia. Eisenhower and his Allied Expeditionary Force (AEF) of Americans, British, and Canadians were simultaneously advancing through France and the Low Countries.

British ground troops were the closest Allied forces to where Josek and I were being held in April,1945—in the rural village of Neu Glassau in the northern province of Schleswig-Holstein. As the Nazis struggled to figure out what to do with all of us, we were desperately praying the British would find us soon.

Assisting their advance were thousands of British bombers under Air Chief Marshal Sir Arthur "Bomber" Harris, who was pursuing a strategic plan to demolish Germany's will to fight. In addition, as close support for armor and infantry, RAF Typhoon fighter-bomber pilots were bombing, rocketing, and machine-gunning trains, trucks, and troops resisting the advance.

In an odd twist, at the same time that Reichsführer Heinrich Himmler was arranging the disposition of the concentration camp prisoners under his control, ordering camp evacuations and contemplating mass murders, he was also, behind Hitler's back, trying to arrange a surrender to Eisenhower. His contact was Count Folke Bernadotte, Vice-Chairman of the Swedish Red Cross. Bernadotte was in Germany trying to negotiate the release of concentration camp prisoners, primarily Scandinavian. He had a fleet of trucks and ships ready to transport them. Ultimately his efforts would touch my life, as Josek and I would get a chance to join his exodus.

As my brother and I struggled to stay alive, day by day, in our own small group of prisoners, larger events in the European Theater also held our fates in their grasp. Their story is our story as well.

■ ■ ■

As you read this narrative, you will hear two voices. The first is that of the twenty-five-year-old concentration camp prisoner I was in May, 1945, describing the attack and its aftermath as they happened. This voice appears at the start of each chapter. The second is that of an older man looking back, who can now provide the historical context and behind-the-scenes information he could not have known at the time. Eugene Pool was instrumental in fleshing out this retrospective voice.

TIME LINE OF
SIGNIFICANT EVENTS

1944

Throughout	*My brother Josek and I are imprisoned at Auschwitz, where I am known as "the Dentist of Auschwitz."*
Jan 6	Soviet armies cross 1939 frontier into Poland.
Jul 24	Soviets liberate the first concentration camp, Majdanek.
Sep 1	SHAEF (Supreme Headquarters Allied Expeditionary Forces) becomes operational on the Continent.
Sep 17	Operation Market-Garden begins.
Sep 23	Operation Market-Garden concludes.
Oct 9	Fourth Moscow Conference begins.
Dec 16	German panzers attack AEF through Ardennes Forest. The Battle of the Bulge begins.

1945

Jan 3	AEF counterattacks.
Jan 7	British and Americans bomb Munich.
Jan 8	Panzers begin to pull back.

Jan 11	*My brother and I leave Auschwitz on our first death march.*
Jan 17	Soviet Army crosses Vistula and captures Warsaw.
Jan 18	*We arrive at Buchenwald and are marched to Dora-Mittelbau.*
Jan 27	Soviets liberate Auschwitz.
Jan 28	The Battle of the Bulge concludes.
Jan 30	Soviet submarine S-13 sinks the *Wilhelm Gustloff.*
Feb 4	The Yalta Conference begins.
Feb 8	The AEF resumes its advance.
Feb 11	Soviet submarine S-13 sinks the *General von Steuben.*
Feb 12	Count Folke Bernadotte and Heinrich Himmler meet for first time.
Feb 13–14	British and Americans bomb Dresden.
Feb 20	Captain Gertz of the *Cap Arcona* shoots himself in Copenhagen.
Feb 21	AEF troops reach the Rhine.
Mar 7	AEF troops cross the Rhine at Remagen.
Mar 12	Bernadotte's "white buses" enter Germany from Denmark.
March	RAF No. 184 squadron becomes the first Typhoon squadron to move to an air base in Germany.
April	RAF Nos. 193, 197, 198, 263, and 609 squadrons move to air bases in Germany.

Apr 2	Bernadotte and Himmler meet again.
Apr 10	*We leave Dora-Mittelbau on our second death march.*
Apr 12	Roosevelt dies.
	Advance elements of U.S. 9th Army reach the Elbe.
Apr 13	*Deutschland* arrives in Neustadt Bay.
Apr 14	*Cap Arcona* arrives in Neustadt Bay.
	Himmler publishes his order that "no prisoner is to fall into enemy hands alive."
	We arrive at Max Schmidt's farm in Neu Glassau, Schleswig-Holstein.
Apr 16	Soviet submarine L-3 sinks the *Goya*.
Apr 18	SS officers meet with Captains Bertram and Jacobsen.
Apr 19	First Neuengamme prisoners arrive in Lübeck.
Apr 20	SS load first prisoners onto the *Thielbek*.
Apr 21	Himmler promises Bernadotte no more Jews will be killed and no more camps will be evacuated.
Apr 24	Himmler asks Bernadotte to arrange a separate surrender to the AEF.
Apr 25	AEF forces cross the Elbe, meeting up with Russian forces.
Apr 26	SS troops load first prisoners onto the *Cap Arcona*.
Apr 28	*Swedish Red Cross refuses to rescue Josek and me.*
Apr 29	Hitler appoints Dönitz the next Führer.

Captain Bertram officially protests the loading of the *Cap Arcona.*

Commandant Pauly completes the evacuation of Neuengamme.

Apr 30   Hitler commits suicide.

May 2   Tugs tow *Thielbek* into Neustadt Bay.

British 6 Commando and 11th Armored Division enter Lübeck.

International Red Cross official P. de Blonay informs General "Pip" Roberts that thousands of prisoners have been loaded onto ships in Neustadt Bay.

The Stutthof Massacre begins.

We leave Neu Glassau at night.

May 3   Early A.M.   Stutthof Massacre ends.

We board the Cap Arcona.

1130   Montgomery receives von Friede-burg, but rejects his offer of surrender.

1135   First RAF sortie to Neustadt Bay, by No. 263 and No. 609 squadrons. Target: *Deutschland.* Planes turn back because of poor visibility.

Midmorning. Major Hans Arnoldson of Swedish Red Cross informs two British officers that prisoners, not Nazi troops, are on ships in Neustadt Bay.

1230	First successful RAF attack on Neustadt Bay, by No. 184. Target: *Deutschland.*
1430	Second RAF attack on Neustadt ` Bay, by No. 198. Targets: *Cap Arcona* and *Thielbek.*
1530	*I leap from* Cap Arcona, *leaving my brother behind.*
1545	Third RAF attack on Neustadt Bay, by No. 263, returning. Target: *Deutschland.*
1550	Fourth RAF attack on Neustadt Bay, by No. 193 and No. 197. Target: *Deutschland.Thielbek* sinks.
1615	*Cap Arcona* capsizes.
	30 AU, 6 Commando, 11th Armored, 15th (Scottish) Division, and other British ground troops enter Neustadt.
	I wade ashore at Neustadt.
1830	*Deutschland* sinks.
1900	British send out rescue boats.
May 4	Morning.	*I am reunited with my brother.*
	Afternoon.	*We depart the area, free men, after four years of captivity and deprivation.*
	1820	Montgomery accepts von Friedeburg's surrender of all Nazi forces in Northwest Germany and Scandnavia.

May 7		British hold memorial ceremony for dead prisoners.
		In Rheims, General Alfred Jodl and other Nazis sign instrument of unconditional surrender of Germany to the Allies.
May 8		In Berlin, German military leaders sign final surrender document.
May 9	0001	World War II officially ends in Europe.

1

No Prisoner Is to Fall into Enemy Hands Alive

MAY 3, 1945. SOMETIME AFTER MIDNIGHT. SCHLESWIG-HOLSTEIN, NORTHWEST GERMANY. We were marching in the dark again. It was too dangerous to travel in the daytime. British warplanes swept over the countryside, bombing and rocketing anything that moved on the roads.

I could see only the heads and shoulders of the five prisoners in the row directly in front of me. There were a hundred or so of us altogether. Although it was early May, the air was cold and damp. Some of the men wore blankets like hoods over their heads to keep warm. Others went bareheaded, wearing just the black-and-white-striped camp jackets and trousers.

My brother Josek was on my left. He was thirty-one, six years older than I was. We shared our mother's dark hair and large eyes and our father's determined mouth, but Josek's face was longer than mine and he was taller as well. On my right walked the Engel twins, Willy and Vikky, from Prague. Our wood-soled shoes, slapping the hard dirt of the backcountry road, made a hollow, rolling sound. A strong smell of manure floated on the air, no doubt from a nearby farm. Occasionally one of the men coughed.

We were in Schleswig-Holstein a rural province on the Baltic coast. Scharführer-SS (Sergeant) Max Schmidt, commandant of our group, and his *kapos*—the privileged prisoners who helped him guard us—had awakened us in the middle of the night. They had driven us out of the big brick barn in which we had been billetted, lined us up, taken roll call, and then marched us off.

Four and a half months earlier—on January 11, to be exact—we had left Auschwitz the same way—without warning, in the cold, in the dark, in rows of five. We had no idea where we were going or what would become of us. We only knew, like everyone, that the Russians were invading Poland. They would soon liberate the camp. The Nazis didn't want us to fall into their hands. We had stories the Nazis didn't want the world to hear.

Reichsführer-SS (Empire Leader), Head of Gestapo, and Interior Minister Heinrich Himmler was responsible for the concentration camps. He would later say, in response to a query from two camp commandants, "No prisoner is to fall into enemy hands alive."

From Auschwitz SS guards had marched us west to a railhead. Hundreds died along the way, if not from exposure or starvation, then from gunshots. The guards executed anyone who couldn't keep up. In the early mornings and evenings, when the light was dim, we had to be careful where we put our feet. Otherwise, we'd trip over the bodies of the unlucky ones, left lying in the road.

They put us in open cattle cars. More died. We threw their bodies into the snow as the train went along. It wouldn't stop. Finally, we arrived at Buchenwald. Our guards marched us to Dora-Mittelbau, a satellite camp, where we spent a couple of months working on the secret V-rockets in caves. As the AEF advanced towards the Rhine, our captors moved us again. They couldn't take us east and they couldn't take us west, so they marched us north, thirty miles or so to the banks of the Elbe, where we boarded open barges. Flowing into Germany from the Giant Mountains of the Czech Republic, the Elbe empties into the North Sea near Cuxhaven. For three days we drifted down the river, passing pretty farmhouses, neat fields, flower-filled gardens, and prosperous-looking barns. Spring was in the air. For once the world looked peaceful and "normal"—like the world we had left behind so long ago. Disembarking outside Hamburg, we marched north again to the village of Neu Glassau, where Schmidt's family had a farm. Ever since, we had lived here in the big brick barn. The Allied armies were pinching the country into an hourglass, and we had been squeezed to the top.

Now we were on the road, in the dark, once more. Where would we end up this time? Where was there left to take us?

"To your right!" shouted a guard. Wrapped in a long wool overcoat, he had a Mauser rifle slung over his shoulder. The men ahead of me slowed, then veered off the road. I followed the silhouettes of their shoulders. I felt soft dirt underfoot, an uneven surface. We went downhill.

Rounding a corner in the dark, I felt suddenly claustrophobic. Shrubs and stunted trees pressed in on both sides; just as abruptly, they fell away. I felt a rush of cold air in my face. I sniffed the deep, unmistakable smell of the sea.

"Halt!" called a guard. The men in front of me stopped, then fanned out, muttering. There was just enough light for me to see we were on a beach. It was narrow, flat, and featureless.

The Nazis had finally run out of places to put us. We stood, literally, on the very edge of Germany.

On the grand scale, it was already clear that Germany had lost the war. Everyone knew it. All of us—prisoners and captors alike—had seen British and American planes for months, and had heard the sound of artillery fire for weeks.

As Nazi Minister of Armaments Albert Speer testified at his postwar trial in Nuremberg:

> The fuel production had been quite inadequate since the beginning of the attacks on fuel plants in May, 1944, and the situation did not improve afterwards. The bombing of our transportation centers had eliminated the Ruhr

[the industrial heartland] as a source of raw material for Germany as early as November, 1944, and with the successful Soviet offensive in the coal areas of Upper Silesia, most of our supply of coal from that region had been cut off since the middle of January, 1945.

Thus we could calculate precisely when the economic set-up must collapse. We had reached a point at which, even if there were a complete cessation of operations on the part of the enemy, the war would soon be lost, since the Reich, because of its lack of coal, was on the verge of an economic collapse.

For my brother Josek and me, one question ruled our lives: having survived the hell of the concentration camps for four long years, could we hold out just a little longer? Having avoided illness, starvation, and shootings, could we now manage to avoid whatever fate the Nazis had planned for us on this godforsaken beach at the edge of the Baltic? Whether it was imprisonment in another camp, transportation to another country, or, finally, our deaths, we could only pray that the Americans or the British—hundreds of miles closer to us than the Russians—would reach us before one last Nazi plan could be carried out. Surely, the airplanes we had watched fly over for so many months would come for us now!

In fact, we wondered what had been keeping the Allies. We knew all about D-day. We'd heard about the Red Army's counterattack against the German forces which had invaded their country. Operation Bagration, which began on June 22, 1944 with 2,000,000 Soviet soldiers, had been a spectacular success.

Pressing on into Poland, the Russians had liberated Majdanek, the first concentration camp to be entered by any of the Allies, on July 24. The camp was a killing center; the Nazis had razed its buildings in an attempt to obliterate any traces of what had gone on there. In April 1942, SS troops had slaughtered 2,800 Jews in a single mass execution. On November 3, 1943, they had machine-gunned another 17,000 Jews to death. It is estimated that of the 500,000 people who passed through Majdanek, 200,000 perished. Approximately 125,000 of that number were Jews. Russian soldiers found thousands of inmates still alive at the camp and, despite the efforts of the SS, ample evidence of the mass murders that had occurred.

On July 31 the Red Army reached the Warsaw suburb of Praga, where Soviet leader Josef Stalin ordered a halt. The very next day, in Warsaw, soldiers of the Polish Home Army rose up against their German occupiers, attacking with home-made Molotov cocktails and antiquated rifles from the 1939 Polish National Army. For sixty-six days, under the direction of a government-in-exile in London, the Home Army fought the Germans. However, by early October, German artillery and aircraft had destroyed the resistance and most of the city. Some 55,000 Poles had died.

The government-in-exile and the British were outraged at Stalin, who had held his troops outside Warsaw while its defenders died and the city burned. Stalin had already been thinking about the postwar world. For his own reasons he wanted the Home Army and Poland's political leadership destroyed. He simply let the Nazis do the job for him.

Stalin's complicity in the destruction of Poland's military and political leadership led to the first crack in the Soviet-Anglo-American alliance and eventually to the Cold War. Stalin's decision also delayed the Red Army's invasion of Germany by a good two months. Josek and I and our fellow prisoners suffered eight unnecessary weeks of starvation, brutality, and danger.

In the west, the AEF had of course established a solid beachhead on the Continent on D-day. However, the Allies had been unable to break out of it. The vigorous assault of the June 6 landing had dissipated into a costly slog through Normandy fields and hedgerows, which the Germans defended with skill and tenacity. Only with the capture of Caen on July 9, the fall of St. Lô on July 18, and the breakthrough at Avranches on July 31 could the AEF sustain its advance. It was not until August 25 that Allied forces liberated Paris.

However, by September 1 the Supreme Headquarters of the AEF (SHAEF) was officially operational on the Continent, with U.S. General Dwight D. Eisenhower assuming command of all

Allied ground forces in the west. The calm, broad-faced, Kansan was charged not only with developing an effective military strategy, but also with handling a cadre of ambitious, high-ranking officers with sizeable egos—among them British Field Marshal Bernard Law Montgomery and U.S. General George S. Patton. Three main army groups confronted the so-called "Siegfried Line" of pillboxes, tank traps, and machine-gun nests the Germans had painstakingly created to protect their country's border. As Ted Ballard of the U.S. Army Center of Military History explains, "in the north, [Field Marshal Bernard Law] Montgomery's 21st British Army Group directed Lt. General Henry Crera's Canadian 1st Army and General Miles Dempsey's 2nd British Army. General Omar N. Bradley's 12th U.S. Army Group occupied the center [and controlled] 9th U.S. Army under Lt. General William Simpson, 1st Army under General Hodges, and General George Patton's 3rd Army. In the south lay General Devers's 6th Army Group, made up of [General] Patch's 7th Army and General Jean de Tassigny's 1st French Army."

On September 11, Patch's 7th Army, crossing the Rhone Valley, connected up with Patton's 3rd Army, "so that a solid wall of Allied forces now stretched from Antwerp to the Swiss border."

Rather than confront the Siegfried Line, the Allies planned to slip into Holland, secure the bridges across its canals and rivers, then sweep around the north end of the fortified barrier. Accordingly, on September 17, Montgomery launched Operation Market-Garden, two separate but connected offensives. Operation Market, the first, was the airborne assault to capture the bridges. Operation Garden was the follow-up advance on the ground, by tanks of 30 Corps and infantry of the British 2nd Army.

Montgomery, the hero of El Alamein in North Africa, was a feisty, energetic, and ambitious leader, if sometimes inclined to be overly fastidious in his preparations for battle. With his clipped moustache, hawk-like nose, piercing eyes, and crisp manner of speaking he could be intimidating as well as charismatic.

As military historian Charles B. MacDonald wrote of Market-Garden,

The airborne attack was designed to lay a carpet of air-borne troops along a narrow corridor extending approximately eighty miles into Holland from Eindhoven northward to Arnhem. . . . The airborne troops were to secure bridges across a number of canals as well as across three major water barriers—the Maas, the Waal (the main downstream branch of the Rhine), and the Neder Rijn (Lower Rhine) Rivers.

The principal objective of the [combined] operation was to get Allied troops across the Rhine. Three main advantages were expected to accrue: cutting the land exit of those Germans remaining in western Holland; outflanking the enemy's frontier defenses, the West Wall or Siegfried Line; and positioning British ground forces for a subsequent drive into Germany along the North German plain.

Dropping by parachute and descending in gliders, the First Allied Airborne Army—comprised of British, American, and Polish forces—landed near the Dutch towns of Eindhoven, Nijmegen, and Arnhem. However, by September 26, just a little more than a week later, these troops were making a bloody retreat. Unknowingly, they had dropped right into the middle of 2nd Panzer Corps. In addition, poor radio communication and bad weather hampered coordination on the ground and delayed air support.

By September 28 the Germans had crushed the Allied operations. The AEF suffered casualties of 17,200 dead, captured, or missing. One Dutch commentator pointed out, "The biggest problem of all probably was the small margin the whole operation had. Everything had to be carried out on a tight schedule and if anything were delayed, the whole plan would fall apart. One setback may have been surmountable and Arnhem would have been reached in time, but that's not what happened."

MacDonald wrote, "The operation was a daring strategic maneuver that failed. That the decision to launch it has not prompted the kind of controversy surrounding other command decisions is somewhat singular. . . ."

On October 9 in Moscow, Stalin, British Prime Minister Winston Churchill, and Averell Harriman, representing President Franklin Roosevelt, convened to discuss the political future of Eastern Europe. At this meeting—the so-called Fourth Moscow Conference—the Soviet Union, the United States, and Great Britain divided Eastern Europe into "spheres of influence," although no one used that term publicly.

Churchill put a proposal on the table before Stalin the very first night, without Harriman present. It is legendary both for its brevity and the speed with which it was accepted. Churchill described the incident in his memoirs:

> The moment was apt for business, so I said, 'Let us settle about our affairs in the Balkans. . . . So far as Britain and Russia are concerned, how would it do for you to have ninety percent predominance in Rumania, for us to have ninety percent of the say in Greece, and go fifty-fifty about Yugoslavia?' While this was being translated, I wrote on a sheet of paper:
>
> | | |
> |---------------------|--------|
> | Rumania | |
> | Russia | 90% |
> | The others | 10% |
> | Greece | |
> | Great Britain | 90% |
> | (in accord with USA) | |
> | Russia | 10% |
> | Yugoslavia | 50-50% |
> | Hungary | 50-50% |
> | Bulgaria | |
> | Russia | 75% |
> | The others | 25% |
>
> I pushed this across to Stalin, who had by then heard the translation. There was a slight pause. Then he took his blue pencil and made a large tick upon it, and passed it

back to us. It was all settled in no more time than it takes
to set down.

Difficulties in Belgium also hampered the AEF's advance. The
British and Americans had captured the Belgian port city of
Antwerp on September 3, 1944. This city was crucial to the Allied
advance because of its extensive docking facilities and its proximity
to the line of advance. Without Antwerp, the Allies had to continue
to use the port of Cherbourg, three hundred fifty miles to their
rear. However, while the Allies held the city of Antwerp, they could
not use the actual port because it was sixty miles inland up the
Schelde estuary and the Nazis still controlled the entrance to
the Schelde. They had entrenched troops and eleven major gun
batteries on Walcheren Island at the mouth of the waterway.

The island was actually below sea level. A protective dike encir-
cled its perimeter. In early October the Allies bombed the dike,
flooding the island. However, the gun batteries remained operational. On November 1, in Operation Infatuate, British and Canadian marines and army troops attacked along the single causeway
connecting Walcheren to the mainland and landed on its beaches.
The Nazis responded with tenacious fighting, but ultimately surrendered on November 8. The Allies suffered 13,000 casualties.
Because the Germans had mined the estuary and deployed U-
boats offshore, the AEF was not able to secure the port until almost three weeks later, on November 28.

The failure of Market-Garden and the costly fight for the port
of Antwerp markedly slowed the AEF's advance. Stephen Ambrose
put it succinctly: "The great offensive of August in France had not
led to victory in Europe. Market-Garden had failed and Antwerp
was not opened in time to do any good." What it meant for Josek
and me at Auschwitz, and for all other inmates, was another long,
hard winter of deprivation and struggle, and the continuing risk of
executions and death marches.

While elements of the Red Army delayed outside Warsaw, the
Soviet advance continued at other points along the eastern front.
On August 31 the Russians took Bucharest, and on September 26,

they entered Estonia. By October 20 they were in Belgrade. On October 23, they crossed the East Prussian border. Two million inhabitants of the German enclave fled their homes and towns, fearful of reprisals. Some 900,000 of these made for Danzig to board transport ships for Copenhagen.

On December 7 Eisenhower met with Montgomery, Bradley, and Patton to plan "an all-out offensive for the early weeks of 1945." The first order of business was to agree on its nature. Eisenhower favored a measured, coordinated advance along the entire front. Montgomery, Bradley, and Patton supported a single spearhead aimed at Berlin, which they believed would bring a quicker end to the war.

Montgomery was particularly insistent. He may have been the Hero of El-Alamein, but he saw himself as the goat of Market-Garden. As one historian put it, "Montgomery wanted a quick end to the war, he wanted the British to bring it about, and he wanted to lead the charge into Berlin personally."

More than just military considerations were involved. Churchill had grown wary of Stalin. His handling of Warsaw and his swift capture of Romania, Estonia, and Hungary revealed a ruthlessness and voraciousness no one had anticipated. Churchill had concluded it would be far better if the AEF took Berlin. And it would be even better if the British took it. Berlin would give Churchill a nice bargaining chip at the end of the war. Plus, whoever entered the city first would be perceived as the victor of the war in Europe. Finally, as military historian Ted Ballard points out, "by 1944 the costs of the war were bankrupting Great Britain; shortening the war [by the quick capture of Berlin] would relieve the overwhelming economic drain."

However, in Eisenhower's view the Nazis, who still had millions of soldiers available, might easily destroy a spearhead. He also estimated that the taking of Berlin would cost some 100,000 casualties (in actuality, he underestimated; most historians agree that the Soviet armies suffered over 70,000 killed and another 230,000 wounded or missing before they took Berlin.) Eisenhower was reluctant to pay such a steep price for a purely symbolic victory. The British, Americans, and Soviets had been debating the postwar structure of Germany since late 1943. They discussed the fate of Berlin in particular at both the Cairo and Tehran Conferences. The city was to go to the USSR. As Eisenhower put it, "Why should we endanger the life of a single American or Briton to capture areas we [would] soon be handing over to the Russians?"

Eisenhower preferred a slow, methodical advance in order to keep his enemy stretched thin and to allow adequate time for fuel and materiel to come down the still very long supply line from Cherbourg. Eisenhower's forces were strong and coordinated. He wanted to keep them that way. A spearhead would separate his troops and expose their flanks. "Unless we get a good natural line for the defensive portions of our long front, we will use up a lot of divisions in defense," he observed. Only when his men were lined up on the Rhine, Germany's western border, in a strong defensive posture, would he feel confident about releasing some divisions for individual offensive initiatives.

Finally, and most importantly, Eisenhower was worried the Nazis were establishing a National Redoubt in the Austrian Tyrol. He had intelligence that they were already stockpiling food and munitions near Innsbruck. There were rumors that they were transporting their advanced weapons there—the V-rockets and jet planes. It would be enormously difficult to get the Germans out of the mountains once they got in. Eisenhower feared an endless protraction of the war by SS units running hit-and-run guerrilla operations, as well as the continued development of weaponry.

According to historian Forrest C. Pogue: "There were disquieting reports, later proved inaccurate, that the Germans were preparing a mountain redoubt in southern Germany and Austria from which they could harry the Allies and prolong the war for months to come. This was a particularly unpleasant prospect for the United States, which wanted to end the war quickly in Europe in order to shift men and supplies to General MacArthur in the Pacific." Committing large numbers of troops to a Berlin spearhead would delay and diminish any advance on the Tyrol.

Ultimately Eisenhower believed the slower, more cautious approach was actually the quickest way to end to the war. The last few months had given him a renewed respect for the Nazi military machine. He had come to feel "that the only way to defeat the Wehrmacht was to destroy it." He saw territorial gains as relatively unimportant. If the Allies defeated the Nazis, they would take over the whole country anyway.

In none of the plans that Eisenhower and his staff discussed were concentration camp prisoners included. We were on our own.

2

WHERE COULD THEY BE TAKING US?

MAY 3, 1945. EARLY HOURS. On the chilly beach, my brother Josek nudged me. "Look."

At the edge of the water a group of SS troops stood talking and smoking. The ends of their cigarettes glowed in the dark. Beside them we could make out half a dozen wooden dinghies, the size of lifeboats, drawn up on the sand. "Are those boats for us?"

I shrugged. "Where could they be taking us?"

"Why do they care anymore, anyway? Hitler's dead," Josek said.

I wondered, too. We had heard he'd killed himself just the day before. The news had been broadcast on our guards' radios; the guards told the kapos, and the kapos told us. However, this event did not seem to have slowed in any way the Nazis' determination to persecute the Jews.

The sky brightened to a flat gray like a gull's wing. As I learned later, we were standing on the edge of Neustadt Bay, named after the nearby town, looking north. Just over two miles wide and one and a half miles long, Neustadt Bay emptied into Lübeck Bay. This body of water in turn emptied into Mecklenburger Bay, flowing into the Baltic Sea some sixty miles north of us. The shoreline which curved away to our left, and west, eventually swung north to form the

Fehmarn Peninsula, the western edge of Lübeck Bay. To our right, the coastline curved east, then north, eighty miles to Warnemünde.

Josek and I took a few steps closer to the water's edge. The pale light reflected off barely perceptible undulations. There was just a breath of wind. Staring out, I could see only a white mist floating on the water. I could see nothing beyond. What lay out there? Another camp? Another country? Our deaths, after all?

I couldn't have felt more forlorn. While of course I was glad to be still alive, I was also filled with tremendous fear and foreboding. So, I knew, was every prisoner on the beach. Why had we been awakened in the middle of the night? What was suddenly so crucial? What new thing had happened—or what order been given?

Huddled with my brother, I could only shiver and wait.

Finally, someone shouted an order. The guards tossed their cigarettes in the water. Calling out, they waved us forward. Our own kapos came up from behind and herded us down the beach. Wading into the freezing water, we climbed into the boats. Our kapos went back up the beach and stood in a group, staring at us. When all of the narrow dinghies were filled, the guards started their engines. One by one, in a ragged line, we chugged off into the mist.

The Allies did know about the *konzentrationslager*—the concentration camps. In fact, at the highest levels they had known for years. As historian Joseph Persico notes, "[As early as] July 10, 1942, John Franklin Carter [a personal intelligence adviser to Roosevelt] delivered to the White House reports written by eyewitnesses to the horrors of daily life in concentration camps in Poland and Lithuania. One account described the mass electrocution of Jews in a place called Belzec. [OSS Chief] Bill Donovan's people contributed further to the catalogue of horrors. His agents interrogated steamship passengers landing in New York, one of whom, a banker who had fled Berlin in November 1941, gave a harrowing account of how the Nazi regime went about rounding up Jews and transporting them to the camps."

Churchill also knew. "Solid intelligence of what was happening to the Jews mounted as Ultra [the Enigma code-breakers] intercepted

Nazi dispatches. Decrypts forwarded to Churchill included a report from Erich von dem Bach-Zelewsi, an SS general operating in occupied Russia [that] '. . . the figure of [Jewish] executions in my area now exceeds 30,000.' "

Yet, as Persico notes, "Curiously, in the stream of secret messages passed directly between [Roosevelt and Churchill], there is no mention of the situation."

In Europe, it seems, some people knew not only about the camps, but also about what went on inside them. A Swedish count, Folke Bernadotte, was Vice-Chairman of the Swedish Red Cross and its de facto head. He would soon get directly involved in the rescue of concentration camp prisoners. In a memoir, he wrote that as early as 1944, people had knowledge of what was going on. Furthermore, they knew what might happen if Germany lost the war. According to Bernadotte, "For some time there had been rumors, impossible to ignore, that the German authorities meant to liquidate the prisoners in concentration camps if there should be a collapse in Germany's defenses, and thus to rid themselves of dangerous witnesses."

As strategic discussions among the AEF generals concluded, it became clear that Eisenhower would have his way. The new year of 1945 would see a slow, carefully coordinated offensive, not a sprint for Berlin. However, as the Allies prepared for their measured advance, they got a rude shock—the biggest, in fact, since they had landed.

On December 16 Hitler launched a vicious surprise attack, Operation Autumn Mist, through Belgium's Ardennes Forest toward Brussels and Antwerp. Two Panzer armies poured out from concealed positions in the Eifel Mountains on the Siegfried Line. Hitler's objective was to split off the British and Canadian armies from their American counterparts, and smash through the resulting gap to Antwerp, recapturing the city. He would also recapture its oil, which his Panzers desperately needed. At the same time he would deny the AEF the ability to shorten its supply lines.

The question for Eisenhower suddenly became not how or when to advance, but whether or not he would have to retreat. The opportunity for our early liberation sank abruptly and the likelihood of thousands more prisoner deaths dramatically increased.

The Battle of the Bulge, named for the buckling of the front, became one of the largest land battles of the entire war, with over a million combatants involved. The Nazis threw twenty-nine divisions against the Allies. Eisenhower responded with thirty-one. The fighting was brutal, the weather bitter. Two particular incidents reflect the ferocity of the fighting and the importance of the engagement.

On December 17 elements of the 1st SS Panzer Division and a group of lightly armed U.S. soldiers met by chance at the Baugnez crossroads just southeast of the town of Malmedy in Belgium. Surrounded by tanks and infantry in large numbers, the American commander surrendered. SS troops herded their prisoners into an adjacent field. As U.S. Army Major Scott T. Glass wrote, after the tanks had moved on, the officer in charge "ordered a tank crew to fire on the U.S. POWs. One shot rang out, then another, and then a fusillade of small arms and machine-gun fire scythed into the U.S. ranks.

"A few POWs bolted, but most fell where they stood—either killed or seriously wounded. German fire cut down almost all who tried to escape before they could run very far. The SS soldiers on the scene roamed among the fallen POWs, shooting or bludgeoning those who showed signs of life.

"Nearly 80 U.S. soldiers died at Baugnez after surrendering. Some, however, managed to elude the Germans. These survivors filtered into the 291st Engineer Battalion positions at Malmedy, giving the [Malmedy Massacre] its name."

The second incident is better known. To stop the Nazi advance, the AEF had to hold two key crossroads in the villages of St. Vith and Bastogne. After heavy fighting, the Allies abandoned St. Vith, but the U.S. 101st Airborne held fast at Bastogne. Completely surrounded, Brigadier General A. C. McAuliffe nonetheless refused to surrender his troops. When the Nazis demanded he do so, he famously replied "Nuts!" The 101st held out until Patton's tanks eventually arrived to throw back the Germans.

On January 1, in support of his ground offensive, Hitler ordered the last German air offensive of the war. Operation Great Blow sent bombers into Belgium, Holland, and France. They destroyed 206 Allied aircraft. However, the Luftwaffe lost 300 of its own airplanes and pilots in the process. While the AEF had ample reserves of both, the Germans did not. In effect, the Luftwaffe had put itself out of business.

On January 3 Montgomery mounted a major counterattack from the north.

On January 7, as a response to Great Blow, British and American warplanes firebombed Munich. They destroyed hundreds of buildings. Ten thousand people died.

On January 8, the stalled 6th SS Panzer Army began to retreat. The tide had turned. Montgomery's response, clearing weather (which allowed the AEF to launch air strikes), and German supply problems had taken their toll.

The failure of Hitler's offensive meant that Germany could now expect a rapid advance on its western, as well as eastern, front. This situation forced the Nazis to make a number of decisions more quickly than they had expected. Among them was what to do with the remaining concentration camps and their thousands of prisoners.

Reichsführer Himmler had overall responsibility for the concentration camps. By early 1945 he had privately concluded that Germany would lose the war. Of course the last thing he wanted was for the Allies to find out about the camps. He decided their buildings and crematoria had to be razed, their records destroyed, and their prisoners "disappeared." Mass executions and evacuations were the methods he chose to achieve this last objective.

The Nazis murdered thousands of prisoners outright in the camps in early 1945. In February SS troops gassed several thousand inmates at Sachsenhausen on the eve of the camp's evacuation. Between the end of January and April they gassed 2,300 women at Ravensbrück. These are just two examples. The prisoners they didn't execute, they evacuated on the infamous "Death Marches." During these forced relocations away from the advancing armies, thousands expired from what the Nazis liked to call "natural causes"—exhaustion, exposure, malnutrition, and over-exertion. If prisoners didn't keep up, guards simply shot them, leaving them by the side of the road.

JANUARY 11, 1945. AUSCHWITZ. Scharführer Schmidt ordered us all out of our barracks. We stood shivering in the cold. Snow covered the ground. After the kapos had destroyed our belongings, left behind on our bunks, Schmidt marched us out of the camp and down a hard, icy road. We headed west, away from the Soviet advance, toward the German interior, with thousands of other prisoners. This was to become the first of two death marches. By this time the Soviet Army was within one hundred miles of the camp.

The march was unbelievably brutal. We were always cold, always starving, always exhausted. Our guards gave us little rest. If one of us stumbled and fell, the SS shot him and left him where he lay. In the early morning and late afternoon, when the light was bad, we had to be very careful where we put our feet. We didn't want to trip over a corpse and fall down ourselves.

I almost did not survive the evacuation from Auschwitz. One day, the lack of food and water, the stress of the march, and the overall debilitation from four years in the camps caught up with me.

We were marching down some nameless country road under the usual cold gray sky. The trees were bare. No living things moved in the snow-covered fields to either side. We had had little food, and just weak coffee to drink. As I stumbled forward with the others over the clumps of frozen snow and the icy, frozen ruts left by farmers' carts, I suddenly became dizzy and faint.

In fact, I would have fallen down if my brother Josek hadn't seen what was happening. Grabbing me with both hands, he held me up. We both knew what would happen if I collapsed. Willy Engel, one of our friends from Prague, had been walking on my other side. At Josek's urging, he now took hold of my right arm. The two of them dragged me forward. My knees sagged beneath me, and I couldn't give them any help. I felt as if I were floating. It was all I could do to stay conscious.

As we marched along in our rows of five, the SS and kapos would walk beside or behind us. Commandant Max Schmidt traveled on a motorcycle. He cruised up and down the line, to ensure that we were orderly and moving along. A farmer's son, Schmidt was just twenty-five, no older than I was. With his curly blond hair, blue eyes, and cherubic face, he was the proverbial poster boy for the Aryan race. Serving in the army was the high point of his life.

As a former dental student, I had found a place in the infirmary at Auschwitz. Like many other soldiers, Schmidt had often come in to have me clean his teeth, and I had found him pleasant enough and easy to talk to. While he seemed to have traces of humanity, I had also been present when he pulled out his Luger and shot dead a prisoner who had been wounded by a guard. Why? He didn't think the man was going to survive. He didn't think the medical personnel should have to bother with him.

Now, as I staggered down the road, Schmidt suddenly pulled up alongside our little group. "What's wrong with the dentist?" he called to my brother.

"He's too weak to walk."

Schmidt frowned. "Hold on, dentist," he cried, and sped off.

In a short time he reappeared with our chief kapo, Joseph Hermann, on the rear seat of his motorcycle. I was too dazed to remember clearly what happened next. Apparently, Hermann got off the motorcycle, strode up next to me, and shoved an open bottle of vodka into my mouth. As the liquid poured down my throat, I felt seared and warmed at the same time. I gasped. Tears sprang to my eyes. As if I had received a hard slap, my head cleared. I could feel my legs again. I could plan steps and take them by myself—if I concentrated.

Hermann climbed back on the motorcycle. Schmidt drove off. I staggered on between Josek and Willy until we reached the next farm, a mile or two ahead, where we stopped for the night.

The next morning, thank God, I was able to walk. My strength had come back. But how strange it was that the man driving me on this death march, Max Schmidt—whose own guards would have shot me if I had fallen down—had saved my life. It was completely insane—like the camps themselves.

■   ■   ■

On January 12, Churchill made a personal appeal to Stalin—whose troops were still sitting outside Warsaw—to resume his advance and cross the Vistula. Doing so would force the Nazis to redeploy soldiers that were fighting British and American troops in the Battle of the Bulge. Although Stalin had not planned to break camp until January 20, he agreed.

By January 16 the AEF front line was back to where it had been before the counter-offensive. However, the AEF's advance—and our potential liberation—had been set back six weeks. The AEF suffered 76,000 casualties, but for the Nazis the attempt was "a daring but [even more] costly failure." German casualties ran to 100,000. In addition, the AEF destroyed 1,600 German aircraft and 600 tanks.

On January 17 the Soviet Army finally crossed the Vistula, capturing Warsaw.

After weeks of marching and three days' travel in freezing, open railway cars, Josek and I arrived at Buchenwald. Many had died during our journey. From Buchenwald we were sent to Dora-Mittelbau, a satellite camp not far away.

Here the Nazis were building their secret V-rockets, the self-guided missiles designed by Werner von Braun, in underground caves and tunnels that could not be seen from the air and bombed.

We were soon assigned to assist in the production of these weapons. However, the inmates who had already been there for a while explained to us that we really didn't have to work—just pretend to sort parts, for instance—until the foreman came around. The feeling throughout the camp was that the end of the war was so near, no one really cared what we did.

On January 27, the Soviet Army liberated Auschwitz. Soldiers found 1,200 extremely ill prisoners who had been abandoned when the camp was evacuated. Auschwitz was one of the first concentration camps to be visited and made known to the wider world through reports and photographs. Over 1.5 million Jews had died there. We had missed the liberation by just over two weeks.

Meanwhile, the Soviet troops which had moved into East Prussia were taking a savage revenge on the people who had invaded their country—regardless of age or gender. One report has it that "Children were shot indiscriminately . . . old men and boys castrated and their eyes gouged out before being killed or burned alive . . . Women were found nailed to barn doors after being stripped naked and gang-raped, their bodies then used for target practice."

In describing the flight of his pregnant sister and other family members, Christian von Krockow writes, "Many, indeed more than many, people were murdered, and many were taken away, never to be seen again. Sometimes we could hardly believe our ears: an elderly couple were chased into the village pond and forced to stay there until they drowned in the icy waters. A man was hitched to a plow and driven until he keeled over, when a burst from a submachine gun finished him off. The proprietor of the Grumbkow estate, Herr von Livonius, had his arms and legs hacked off and was thrown, still alive, to the pigs."

Such were the brutalities the now-victorious Soviets unleashed on the Germans.

American and British air forces continued to pound Germany in the aggressive air campaign intended to hammer the country into submission. On one day alone, Allied planes flew 11,000 sorties. Air Chief Marshal Harris, Commander in Chief of British Bomber Command, explained that his goal was nothing less than "the progressive destruction and dislocation of the German military, industrial, and economic system, and the undermining of the morale of the German people to a point where their capacity for armed resistance is fatally weakened."

On January 30, Soviet submarine S-13 torpedoed the passenger ship SS *Wilhelm Gustloff*, en route from Gdynia, near Danzig, to Kiel, in Schleswig-Holstein. Normally, the *Gustloff* carried a crew of 400 and 1,465 passengers, but that night she was overloaded by a factor of three with East Prussian refugees fleeing the Soviets. Because of the bad weather, the captain had fully illuminated the ship to make her visible to other vessels. This also made her an easy target. She sank in just fifteen minutes. Between seven and eight thousand people perished in the bitterly cold Baltic. In maritime history, only this tragedy compares in lives lost with the one that my comrades and I were to suffer on May 3.

On February 4, Churchill, Roosevelt, and Stalin met at the former palace of Czar Nicholas at Yalta in the Crimea to coordinate their offensives and discuss Europe's postwar fate. France's leader, General Charles de Gaulle, was not invited. Churchill's objective was to prevent the USSR from occupying the Balkans and too much of Germany. Roosevelt wanted only to bring his troops home as soon as possible and keep out of what he foresaw as a postwar political morass in Europe. Stalin's goal was to get himself a free hand in Eastern Europe.

Churchill could not get support from a frail, and, he felt, naïve Roosevelt. In the end, "the Big Three" simply confirmed what they had discussed before. The USSR would take over Berlin and control of the eastern half of Germany upon its surrender. The Soviets would also be in charge of Poland. The rest of Germany would be divided into three zones, controlled by the U.S., Great Britain, and France. These powers would administer Berlin jointly with the Soviets.

As military historian Forrest Pogue has written, "The zones had been outlined, along general lines suggested by the British, by the European Advisory Commission (EAC) as early as January 1944. The United States and Great Britain had agreed on the main proposals at the Quebec Conference in September 1944 and had settled everything except the control of the Bremen-Bremerhaven enclave when their representatives met at Malta in January 1945 on their way to the Yalta Conference. The Soviet Union accepted the EAC recommendations at Yalta in early February 1945, and the fact that zones of occupation had been established was announced at the close of the meeting."

Critics later accused Roosevelt of a "sell-out" of Eastern Europe. The tired, ailing President argued that the United Nations, which was to be established after the war, was the proper forum for dealing with Stalin. However, to Adolf Berle, one of his close advisers, Roosevelt privately admitted, "I didn't say the result was good. I said it was the best I could do."

Stalin won his free hand in Eastern Europe, as well as additional territories in the Far East—including Outer Mongolia, South Sakhalin Island, and the Kuriles. In return, on August 8 he declared war on Japan in support of the U.S. and Great Britain.

3

SPECIAL INSTRUCTIONS IN CASE OF WAR

MAY 3, 1945. EARLY HOURS. I could barely see the bow of the dinghy in which I was riding. Out over the cold bay, the mist had become a thick fog. Only the wakes of the boats ahead told me they even existed. As I sat on the hard wet bench, my wool camp uniform grew soggier and heavier. Jerked back and forth by the motion of the boat, I stared into the gloom, desperate for a clue to my fate.

Then suddenly, I felt a change. The air ahead darkened, as if a huge stain were spreading through the fog. This darkness loomed up and up, until it seemed as if it would swallow us. Our boats slowed. Above I saw the broad, sloping stern of a gigantic ship emerge from the mist. Towering over us, the ship utterly dwarfed our little dinghies. Her steel sides were painted battleship gray. Streaks of rust ran like long dirty fingers down into the water.

As we drifted closer, I counted four rows of portholes, then two more rows of rectangular windows. Above these were several open decks, one of them hung with lifeboats. The vessel was a passenger ship, an ocean liner, colossal in size. I had never seen such a ship in my life—not even in pictures.

Its name was painted in white capital letters as tall as a man across the stern: CAP ARCONA. I had no idea that the words referred to a famous, cliff-strewn cape jutting out into the Baltic some five hundred miles to the northeast. I had no idea that this gigantic vessel was the battle-weary, worn-out shadow of what was once one of the greatest ocean liners in the world. I could never have imagined such a ship could be my home—even temporarily—let alone, possibly, my tomb.

The area around the *Cap Arcona* was eerily quiet. The bay was still windless and flat, the fog still thick. Only the noise of our idling engines, echoing off the hull, disturbed the scene. Finally, our boatmen shut off the motors. As the last echoes died, we heard a deep voice, coming through a bullhorn from high above. The words were spaced carefully. We could easily make them out.

"ARE—YOU—BRINGING—ME—MORE—PRISONERS?"

"Yes! Exactly!" called up the SS guard in charge, his voice magnified and reverberating in the stillness.

"Well, I refuse to take any more," came the response. "We are already dangerously overloaded."

The SS guard would not take no for an answer. Arguing back and forth, the two shouted at each other as we huddled in the darkness, shivering. Finally, swearing, our guard ordered our boats back to the beach.

It was now clear where our captors intended to take us. It wasn't yet clear if they would be successful.

The ship we left behind was not just any ship. Known as the "Queen of the South Atlantic" in her heyday—from 1927 to 1939—the *Cap Arcona* carried over 50,000 passengers back and forth between Germany and South America. She was the fastest in her class, and fitted out with every luxury.

A contemporary observer notes, "For those of us who did not grow up in the ocean liner age, it is hard to appreciate the extent to which liners before the War were viewed as symbols of national pride and achievement. Hitler as much as anyone viewed liners as a means of state propaganda, and . . . the captains of pre-War liners were treated as national heroes whose names were household knowledge."

On August 25, 1939, the "Queen of the South Atlantic" abruptly lost her crown. Just as the *Cap Arcona* was entering the mouth of the Elbe, returning from a South American cruise, her captain received a coded radio transmission. Message QWA 7 was "special instructions in case of war." The German navy was commandeering her. She went directly into dry dock, where workers painted her black hull and white superstructure a uniform gray.

By November 29 she was tied up to a quay in the Baltic port of Gdynia, near Danzig, in occupied Poland. There she remained for the next six years, providing floating accommodations for U-boat commanders, civilian VIPs, and soldiers—in essence, a floating hotel. Troops spread out their rifles and gear in her staterooms and clumped through her dining rooms in their muddy boots.

The only bit of variety came in 1942, when Minister of Propaganda and Public Information Joseph Goebbels decided to make a film, to be called *The Sinking of the* Titanic. As a member of the *Titanic* Historical Society has noted, "the epic theme of a great ship going down because of British pigheadedness appealed to Goebbels, and as a propaganda spectacle the subject could hardly be bettered." It would feature a German officer who kept his head while all about him people were losing theirs. Goebbels chose the *Cap Arcona* for the set.

He also appointed Herbert Selpin, an experienced filmmaker, to direct. However, the German officers assigned to the *Cap Arcona* interfered with his shooting, ignoring his timetable and running off with his actresses. Their arrogance infuriated Selpin. When he finally exploded to an aide that "a decoration must certainly be awarded for the number of actresses seduced," Goebbels summoned him to Berlin. Selpin would neither recant nor apologize. Charging him with "verbal treason," Goebbels threw him into jail. Two days later, SS officials announced he had "committed suicide" in his cell.

In his book, *Film and the Third Reich*, David Stuart Hull clarifies: "Sometime near midnight on Friday, July 31, 1942 . . . two guards went to Selpin's cell and proceeded to tie his suspenders to the bars of the window high in the ceiling. They brought in a bench. They told Selpin to stand on it and grasp the bars, then tied the suspenders around his neck and took the bench away. When the unfortunate man could no longer hold on, he was strangled to death."

Another director, Werner Klinger, completed the film. However, when Goebbels saw the final cut, he decided not to release the movie. The luxurious shipboard life portrayed by the actors presented too harsh a contrast to the reduced conditions in which wartime Germans were actually living. The scenes of terror, death, and despair were too close to what German civilians were actually experiencing when the Allies bombed their cities. Only years after the war did the movie reach a public screen.

On January 31, 1945, the navy reactivated the *Cap Arcona*, putting her into service ferrying civilian refugees from East Prussia, wounded German soldiers from the eastern front, and other Nazi personnel to the safety of Copenhagen. She was joined by other former passenger liners, including the 21,046-ton *Deutschland* of the Hamburg-Amerika Line. These trips were nothing like the luxury cruises of the past. The captains simply crowded on as many people as they could. On one trip, two thousand women and children bedded down in the Grand Salon of the *Cap Arcona*. The crossings were also extremely dangerous. All of the bays in the area were mined. Russian submarines haunted the shipping lanes.

On February 8, the AEF finally resumed its advance, following Eisenhower's vision. The coordinated, measured offensive had three branches. Patton's 3rd Army rolled south to block the establishment of the National Redoubt in the Tyrol. General Bradley led the 1st and 9th Armies east towards the Rhine. His priorities were to establish a bridgehead across the river and to dismantle the German war machine as he went. Montgomery headed north with the British 2nd Army, toward the Baltic port of Lübeck. If the British could not be the first to Berlin, they would be the first to the Baltic. Sealing off the Jutland Peninsula, they would prevent the Soviets from taking Denmark and establishing a presence too close to England. Also going north was the 1st Canadian Army, making for the Netherlands.

The air campaign continued. British Bomber Command flew twenty-six major assaults in the first four months of 1945. Max Hastings, an expert on Bomber Command, wrote, "American airmen joined wholeheartedly with the British in devastating the last remaining undestroyed cities of Germany, because to leave the great forces idle on the ground would have been an intolerable alternative." Harris stated, "Bombing anything in Germany is better than bombing nothing."

Bonn, Chemnitz, Dortmund, Kassel, Mainz, Mannheim, Munich, Nuremberg, Wiesbaden, and Worms were among the cities bombed. "Night after night the huge palls of smoke and fire rose from the cities," wrote one historian.

In the early morning of February 11, S-13, the same Soviet submarine which had sunk the *Gustloff* torpedoed the 14,666-ton SS *General Steuben*, a hospital ship en route from Gdynia to Copenhagen with wounded soldiers and civilian refugees. The sub came across her at almost the same location that she had found the *Gustloff*. Two of her torpedoes pierced the *Steuben's* hull. The ship went down in seven minutes, taking 3,500 with her.

On February 12, Count Folke Bernadotte of the Swedish Red Cross made the first of several visits to Germany to try to negotiate the release of concentration camp prisoners. His efforts would give Josek and me our first real chance of escape in four years.

A nephew of King Gustav V, Bernadotte was tall and clean-cut, an imposing figure with a polished diplomatic manner. A contemporary journalist said of him, "It is difficult to imagine a person in that situation who would have been more suitable as a negotiator, expedition leader, and intermediary. As a negotiator, Bernadotte was simultaneously calm, inventive, patient, and alert."

Bernadotte came particularly to see Himmler. They met at the Reichsführer's headquarters at Hohen-Lüchen, fifty miles north of Berlin. On the surface Bernadotte's trip was "ostensibly on behalf of a Swedish Red Cross team seeking to repatriate Swedish-born women who had married Germans but since lost touch with them. [However,] his real purpose was to bargain with Himmler for the release of prisoners (especially Scandinavian) from the concentration camps." In this effort, Bernadotte was officially supported by the Swedish Minister for Foreign Affairs, Christian Günther, and unofficially by Gilel Storch, the representative in Sweden of the World Jewish Congress. Bernadotte had already worked with Storch on the transport of some 70,000 food parcels to Jewish prisoners in the camps.

In his memoir, *The Curtain Falls*, Bernadotte describes meeting Himmler:

> I suddenly saw him before me in the green *Waffen-schutzstaffel* [Waffen-SS] uniform; without any decorations and wearing horn-rimmed spectacles, he looked a typical unimportant official, and one would certainly have passed him in the street without noticing him. He had small, well-shaped, and delicate hands, and they were carefully manicured, although this was forbidden by the SS. He was, to my surprise, extremely affable. He gave evidence of a sense of humor, tending rather to the macabre. Frequently he introduced a joke when conversation was threatening to become awkward or heavy.

In the background loomed a recently failed attempt to relocate Jewish prisoners that Jean-Marie Musy, former President of Switzerland, had tried to arrange. "[Musy] had come to an agreement with Himmler whereby the Jews interned at Theresienstadt should be transported to Switzerland en route to the United States. The foreign press got wind of it and published the facts. This was reported to Hitler by one of his press observers, and Himmler was summoned to appear before the Führer. Asked what concessions Germany had obtained in the exchange, Himmler replied that Germany had obtained nothing at all, whereupon Hitler had one of his seizures of rage and forbade any future transportations of this kind."

Musy did succeed in arranging the transport of 1,200 Jews from Theresienstadt to Switzerland on February 8. But his hopes of following up could not be realized.

Bernadotte made a specific request of Himmler—that Norwegians and Danes "be released for internment in Sweden." The Reichsführer responded that he could not entertain the request unless Norwegian and Danish resistance fighters agreed to stop their efforts at sabotage. He wanted a quid pro quo with which to mollify Hitler. Said Bernadotte, "I told Himmler that the concession he had mentioned was quite unthinkable." Eventually Himmler withdrew his demand. It was agreed that "the Norwegians and Danes in question should be collected into two camps, one for each group. [Himmler] also agreed that the aged, the sick, and mothers should be allowed to return to Norway after having been assembled in the camps. He did not even raise any objection to the Swedish Red Cross staffs being admitted to the camps to assist in the collection of the prisoners. The movements would be carried out by a convoy of Red Cross vehicles supplied by the Swedes."

However, the two men had different ideas about the numbers of prisoners involved. Bernadotte imagined gathering "somewhere around thirteen thousand"; Himmler, "[not] more than two or three thousand."

At the end of the meeting Bernadotte presented Himmler with a seventeenth-century Swedish work on Scandinavian runic inscriptions, a gift which the German received with great pleasure.

Also on February 12, the 11th Armored—the famous "Black Bull" regiment—along with other elements of the British army, took the town of Cleve, just a few miles west of the Rhine.

On the night of February 13 a total of 796 British Lancaster bombers dropped 1,478 tons of high explosive bombs and 1,182 tons of incendiary bombs on Dresden, in two waves three hours apart. The next night, 311 American B-17's bombed the city. Overall, between 30,000 and 70,000 people died—mainly, as it turned out, women, children, elderly men, and Allied prisoners of war from the nearby Muehlberg concentration camp. Pilots reported seeing the ground lit up as if it were daylight.

On February 17 a war correspondent at SHAEF filed a dispatch stating that a briefing officer had told him Allied air chiefs had made the decision to adopt deliberate terror bombing of German population centers as a ruthless expedient for hastening the end of the war. The report was widely publicized in America, but not in Great Britain. Nonetheless one of Bomber Command's most persistent critics, Richard Stokes, raised the issue in the House of Commons, quoting a report in the *Manchester Guardian* about the Dresden firestorm. He asked whether "terror bombing" was now official British policy.

Meanwhile, German ships continued to make the overcrowded, dangerous runs from Poland to Denmark. The stress was intense for the officers and crews involved—too intense for some, in fact. On the night of February 20, Johannes Gertz, captain of the *Cap Arcona*, shot himself in his cabin in Copenhagen, unable to face the trip back to Gdynia. Captain Heinrich Bertram, commander of the SS *Monte Rosa* and a stocky, square-jawed career professional with a steady gaze, replaced him.

That same day Folke Bernadotte lunched with General Walter Schellenberg, a close aide of Himmler, who confirmed the February 12 agreement to release the Scandinavian prisoners. They would assemble at Neuengamme concentration camp, just south of Hamburg. Bernadotte "promised to endeavor to have [his] Red Cross column ready at Warnemünde [on the Baltic coast near Rostock] ten days later."

On March 4, 6 and 45 British Commando reached the town of Well, on the Rhine, as part of Operation Veritable. They found all the houses empty. On March 6, the 11th Armored captured the town of Goch, just ten miles short of the Rhine. However, the Black Bulls were unable to cross the river because the Germans had blown up all the bridges.

There were now several Allied units on the west bank of the Rhine, no more than 250 miles from Neustadt.

Historians Denis and Shelagh Whitaker describe what happened next. "On March 7 Eisenhower benefited from a remarkable bit of luck. While the U.S. 9th Armored Division was rumbling toward the town of Remagen, a German prisoner in its hands warned his captors that at precisely 4:00 P.M. that afternoon, a Nazi demolition crew planned to blow up the Remagen bridge.

"The Americans raced to seize it. Although two demolition charges exploded with minor damage, they captured the span intact, crossed it, and established a strongpoint on the other side of Hitler's last natural defense in the West." Holding off counterattacks, the Allies poured across this bridge for ten days before it finally collapsed from overloading.

Still, the bridge could not have handled a large, sustained crossing. "Remagen was in near-impossible terrain [wooded, craggy] for the massive armored breakout that the Allies needed," explain the Whitakers.

At or about this same time, Himmler apparently received an order from Hitler "to destroy the concentration camps and their inmates rather than allow them to fall into enemy hands."

On March 10, the 11th Armored and other units captured Wesel-on-the-Rhine. Now, for all intents and purposes, "all organized resistance west of the Rhine had ceased." On March 12, the first "white buses" of Bernadotte's rescue mission crossed the Danish border into Germany. Bernadotte himself accompanied them. The convoy consisted of three platoons of twelve buses each and one platoon of twelve trucks. The vehicles were painted white with red crosses.

Colonel Gottfrid Björck was in charge. The convoy reached its destination, Schloss Friedrichsruh, near Lübeck, at dusk. Here a telephone message from Obergruppenführer-SS Ernst Kaltenbrunner, Chief of Reich Security Police and a Hitler confidante, was waiting. He objected to the transfer. According to Bernadotte, in Kaltenbrunner's view, "if the program were sanctioned, neutral representatives would obtain far too intimate a view of the conditions in the various camps, the long and carefully preserved secret of their horrors would be revealed, and the last remnants of Nazi prestige would vanish."

On March 19 Hitler sent a powerful message to his territorial commanders or gauleiters, "instructing them on the approach of the enemy to destroy everything in their path, all factories and utilities, power stations, water- and gas-works, dams, all transport and communication facilities and rolling stock. . . ." It was a desperate order that would be interpreted to include concentration camps and their inmates as well. In the actual event, many gauleiters would resist or undercut it, not because of concern for the prisoners, but for love of their homeland.

On March 22, Patton crossed the Rhine at Oppenheim, 150 miles south of the town of Wesel, where the main Allied thrust was to take place the very next night. His action was not a significant military event. Patton made the crossing just to beat Montgomery across the highly symbolic river. In his official announcement, he said: "Without benefit of airborne drop, without benefit of the United States *or* the British Navy and *not* having laid down the greatest smoke screen in the history of modern war, and without either a three months' build-up of supplies *or* a whole extra American army, and with no preliminary bombardment, and finally without even a code word, Lieutenant General Patton and the Third United States Army crossed the Rhine yesterday."

Operation Plunder, the full-scale Allied crossing of the Rhine, launched the next day at 9:00 P.M. with both amphibious and airborne components.

British 1st Special Services Brigade (3, 6, 45, and 46 Commando) was the first element to cross the Rhine at Wesel, in four open "Buffalo" amphibious boats. Its objective was to capture the town and secure the bridgehead. Each Buffalo carried twenty-eight soldiers. Storm Boats and DUKWs [front-wheel drive amphibious utility trucks] followed. A commando who was there described the scene: "[T]he slim ribbon that was the Rhine became almost hidden with the reddish bursts of thousands of shells, each of which left thick, weaving clouds of smoke. Away to the right, around Wesel, it seemed as if thousands of candles had been lighted and suspended like so many fairy lights over the town as orange-colored tracer shells from light anti-aircraft guns curved in a series of graceful parabola towards their targets."

There was a double sense of history to the event. Historian Sir Basil Liddell-Hart noted, "The same flag which Lieut.-Colonel E. J. Carter [had] carried on the leading armored-car to reach the Rhine at the end of World War I was flown by Lieut.-Colonel A. Jolly in one of the first Buffaloes to reach the east bank of the Rhine in World War II.

"In all, about 120 D.D. [water-proofed, floatable, duplex-drive amphibious] Sherman tanks accompanied the assaulting infantry across the Rhine."

At 2:00 A.M. the 11th Armored followed by pontoon bridge. By 10:00 the next morning, over 2,500 paratroopers from the 17th U.S. and 6th British airborne divisions had dropped onto the eastern bank of the Rhine.

Brigadier General Mills-Roberts of the 1st Commando Brigade wrote in overview, "The River Rhine was the last great water barrier in Europe. Once the Rhine had been crossed by 21 Army group, the enemy fought a delaying action across the North German Plain. It was now virtually impossible for them to halt the Allied advance, but every German soldier had been told that every day, and indeed every hour, of delay was of vital importance—it would give the Führer time to end the war with a new and secret 'V' weapon."

Meanwhile, Josek and I were still at Dora-Mittelbau, underground most of the day, feigning work, waiting, and praying.

4

THE QUEEN OF THE SOUTH ATLANTIC

MAY 3, 1945. JUST BEFORE DAWN. Once back at the beach, we sat in the dinghies and waited. The SS guard who had argued with the captain of the *Cap Arcona* went ashore to report to his superior. The officer, a captain, raged at him, then climbed into one of the boats himself and ordered us all back out. We returned to the *Cap Arcona*. The captain reappeared. We waited some more. This time rank prevailed, and a deal was struck. We would be taken aboard, but no more prisoners could be brought out.

A fellow inmate later testified, "Prisoners who could not be taken aboard the ship were shot by SS guards in the presence of the population of Neustadt." But I know nothing about that.

How were we to get aboard? I found out when sailors threw a single flimsy rope ladder over the side. The dinghies drew close. Our guards ordered us up the ladder. Of course, we protested. The side of the ship was six or seven stories high. We were so weak. But with blows the guards literally drove us over the sides of the dinghies. We had no choice.

We barely managed the climb. The ladder swung back and forth, raking our knees and knuckles against the hull. The feet of the man above were always slipping down into the face of the man below.

The wet ropes cut our hands. It seemed as if our arms, which had to bear most of our weight, would tear from our shoulders.

Somehow we made it to the top. Sailors hauled us onto the slippery steel of what I later learned was the Promenade Deck. Dawn had come, and we could now fully appreciate the size of the ship. Hands bleeding and shoulders burning, nonetheless we gaped. The view over the side was astonishing. Above us soared three smokestacks, each over fifty feet tall. When everyone was finally up, a sailor ordered us to follow him forward along the deck.

We passed a long line of windows. Because of the reflections, I couldn't see what was inside. The sailor stopped at a doorway. As I stepped through behind the others, I found myself in muffled silence at the top of a broad, carpeted staircase. The railing I grasped was solid mahogany, its fittings polished brass. The atmosphere was of complete gentility—the very opposite of the world I had been living in for so long. Below me lay the most elegant dining room I had ever seen.

It appeared to be at least a hundred and fifty feet long by fifty feet wide. Soaring Palladian windows pierced the two long walls. Chandeliers hung from the double-height ceiling, while bronze sconces ornamented the walls, which were clad in green silk. Persian carpets covered the parquet floor. At the far end of the room I saw a rich tapestry depicting a fanciful landscape with feathery trees and jagged mountains. Rows of mahogany tables appointed with leather armchairs completed the scene.

Descending the stairway, I paused on a broad landing. Beside me stood a carved wood relief of a nymph, naked and twice life-size. One hip thrust out, she coyly stroked an amphora at her side. I couldn't believe it! In the space of just a few minutes I had come from hanging over the side of this ship, fighting for my life, to strolling through what appeared to be the interior of a luxury hotel.

As we walked hesitantly across the room, it was not hard to imagine the tables covered with snow-white damask tablecloths, waiters in tuxedos emerging from the kitchen with steaming plates of meats and vegetables, while already well-nourished diners chatted pleasantly in their evening wear as they clinked glasses of sparkling Riesling. Ironically, what had once been a ship of the greatest comfort and luxury was about to become the home of concentration camp prisoners who had known the greatest deprivation and suffering.

The *Cap Arcona*'s history was illustrious. The famous Hamburg yard of Blohm & Voss had built the ship. Established in 1877, the firm had already launched 429 large vessels. The Hamburg-Südamerika Line, one of the three largest shipping concerns in Germany, commissioned the *Cap Arcona*. During the 1920s, Hamburg-Süd had monopolized the routes to South America, transporting both middle-class emigrants and upper-class vacationers. The soft air, warm breezes, and benevolent sunshine provided a welcome contrast to German weather. Hamburg-Süd's ships visited La Plata, Buenos Aires, and Rio de Janeiro, among other ports.

But while Hamburg-Süd had been in business since the nineteenth century, World War I almost destroyed the company. The Allies took all of its ships as war reparations. The company had to rebuild itself completely. Beginning with small schooners and gradually adding larger ships, Hamburg-Süd did mange to resurrect itself. The *Cap Arcona* represented the culmination of this effort. The huge, luxurious liner, faster than any similar vessel and the fourth-largest ship in German hands, was the sign that Hamburg-Süd had regained its position in world shipping.

Her launching on May 14, 1927 was a grand occasion. Standing on an elevated platform by the ship's bow, Beatrice Amsic, daughter of the head of Hamburg-Süd, read a flamboyant declaration: "Out of the waves of the Ostsee rises in the north the lively isle Rugen, a rock crowned by a lighthouse, the most important landmark on the Ostsee, whose light shines far across the sea. The name of this rock, the only cape that adorns the coast of Germany, the 'Cap Arcona,' shall be your name. May you from now on, in honor of our Fatherland and for the pleasure of your Company, cross the ocean and be a link between the Old and the New Worlds."

Then Amsic swung a bottle of champagne against the cold steel. With thousands looking on, the great ship slid down the ways with a groan and splashed into Hamburg Harbor, to a chorus of resounding cheers.

The *Cap Arcona* was 676 feet long. She had a beam of 84 feet and displaced 27,560 gross tons. Measuring 189 feet high from keel to mast-top, she carried steam turbines that could generate 24,000 horsepower and a cruising speed of 20 knots. She carried 1,315 passengers—575 in first class, 275 in second class, and 465 in third class. Featured in photographs, postcards, and glamorous travel posters—many of which are still in circulation on the Internet—she enjoyed a worldwide reputation. With black topsides, a bright white superstructure, and three 56-foot funnels with crimson caps, she was instantly recognizable at sea.

On November 19, 1927, just six months after her launching, she left Hamburg on her maiden voyage to Argentina. Truly "a floating palace," she boasted nine decks, the three uppermost of which were devoted entirely to recreation. The Promenade Deck offered 1/5 of a mile of circumference to stroll. The Boat Deck just above, on which the lifeboats hung, featured chaise lounges and wicker armchairs. At the very top, the open-air Sports Deck had a tennis court and several shuffleboard lanes.

When the *Cap Arcona* reached the sunny waters of the South Atlantic, waiters in white coats emerged to serve tea, cakes, lemonade, and stronger drinks to lounging passengers in ascots, scarves, and dark glasses. There was a luxurious ratio of two staff to each guest. The more vigorous passengers could not only play tennis and shuffleboard, but also swim in the heated indoor pool, decorated with a triple-tiered fountain and a glazed terra-cotta relief of mermaids.

A smoking room with a marble fireplace could be found on the Promenade Deck in addition to the Grand Salon, the first-class dining room into which I had stepped when I first arrived on the ship. Two potted palms, as well as the maître d', stood at the foot of the staircase. The tapestry at the far end of the room, as well as the two others in the Salon, were by the house of Gobelin. With a total area of 7,852 square feet, the room could seat 436 passengers at one time.

The staterooms were suites, with bedrooms, sitting rooms, WCs, and full baths. Each sitting room was furnished with a sofa and two armchairs covered in silk. The lavishly papered walls were hung with oils of European landscapes.

Called by many effusive names—not only "The Queen of the South Atlantic," but also "the Pearl of the Atlantic," "the Flower of the Atlantic," and "The Lucky Lady"—the *Cap Arcona* carried the rich and famous back and forth between Germany and South America for twelve years.

Among her passengers was a wealthy Argentinean woman traveling with fourteen dogs. For their comfort she booked two first-class cabins. A Brazilian family brought along its own cow and chickens, so both parents and children could enjoy fresh eggs and milk for breakfast. Important German actors and actresses—and even the American film star, Clark Gable—made voyages on the ship.

A typical day for a First Class passenger on the *Cap Arcona* began with a lavish spread in the Breakfast Room, followed by a stroll on the Promenade Deck. From there one might see a seaplane landing, bringing the mail (the *Cap Arcona* had its own postmark). After a lavish lunch in the Grand Salon, one might exert oneself on the Sports Deck, swim, or bet on one of the outdoor horse races, in which stewards advanced wooden "ponies" at the roll of dice.

After a late-afternoon tea, British-style, one would retire to one's stateroom to dress for dinner, gentlemen in tuxedos and ladies in evening gowns. Dinner, also in the Grand Salon, was an elaborate affair, with selections from a lengthy menu. Afterwards, light waltzing to Strauss melodies could be followed by a final turn on deck, this time in the moonlight, before retiring. Without a doubt, the *Cap Arcona* provided its passengers with the height of luxury.

As the AEF continued its advance into Germany, squadrons of RAF Typhoon fighter-bombers followed, providing close air support, as they had first in France, then in Holland and Belgium. Their pilots were experienced and effective. Now, as quickly as they could, the squadrons took over the German air bases abandoned by the fleeing Nazis. These fields put them in reach of the Baltic—and Neustadt Bay.

As RAF historians Denis Richards and Hilary Saunders explain, "[T]he capture of airfields [was] one of the major objects of the Army. Such operations were very necessary, for . . . if, as was hoped, the advance would be rapid, it might not be possible for [2nd Tactical Air Force] to give full support unless it could be provided with the requisite number of forward airfields."

The No. 184 Squadron (its motto, *nihil impenetrabile*—"nothing impenetrable"), claimed to be the first squadron based on German soil in World War Two. It moved to Hustedt, just ninety miles south of Neustadt Bay, in late March. No. 184 had received its first Typhoons in December, 1943; moved to Normandy in late June, 1944; and supported the AEF in the Netherlands. Derek Stevenson, who would later play an important role on May 3, was Squadron Leader.

On March 27 Bernadotte received permission from Foreign Minister Günther to try to arrange the release of "a number of Jews," Norwegian and Danish, in addition to the prisoners whose transfers he had already negotiated. This was good news.

However, in London there was bad news—for Churchill. On March 28, in reaction to private and public criticism, Churchill had drafted a telegram to his Chiefs of Staff:

> It seems to me that the moment has come when the question of bombing of German cities simply for the sake of increasing the terror, though under other pretexts, should be reviewed. Otherwise we shall come into control of an utterly ruined land. We shall not, for instance, be able to get housing materials out of Germany for our own needs because some temporary provision would have to be made for the Germans themselves. The destruction of Dresden remains a serious query against the conduct of Allied bombing. I am of the opinion that military objectives must henceforward be more strictly studied in our own interests rather than that of the enemy.
>
> The Foreign Secretary has spoken to me on this subject, and I feel the need for more precise concentration

upon military objectives, such as oil and communications behind the immediate battle-zone, rather than on more acts of terror and wanton destruction, however impressive.

Max Hastings wrote, "It is impossible to regard this memorandum as anything other than a calculated attempt by the Prime Minister to distance himself from the bombing of Dresden and the rising controversy surrounding area bombing."

The document, which ignored Churchill's long-term support for the area bombing strategy and his own personal role in arranging the Dresden attack, so shocked the Chiefs of Staff that two of them urged the Prime Minister to withdraw it. On April 1 Churchill backed off, substituting a much more guarded (and acceptable) note, omitting the word "terror."

The Chiefs of Staff were not, as a group, eager to restrict or curtail bombing, since they agreed that "the Baltic and North Sea ports were of [great] importance to eliminate the dangers of another U-boat offensive as well as the liberation of Denmark and Norway, which contained substantial enemy forces, or might more realistically harbor the enemy's last main point of resistance."

Harris himself immediately wrote to Air Marshal Sir Norman Bottomley, stating: "The accusation that we bombed German cities 'with the only intention to create terror, and our offensive to will acts of pure terror and mean destruction' is an insult to the bombing policy of the ministry as well as to the way the Bomber Command enacted such." Furthermore, he said, "I would not regard the whole of the remaining cities of Germany as worth the bones of one British grenadier."

Harris's unequivocal position made him few friends. The stocky, blunt-speaking Air Chief Marshal is the only important World War II commander Great Britain did not honor with a statue after the war. Having sent emissaries to the funeral services of all the important Allied leaders, the Germans sent none to his.

On March 30 the Soviets captured Danzig. This meant the end of evacuations by sea from Gdynia. Captain Bertram had just guided the *Cap Arcona* from Poland to Denmark on her third voyage across the Baltic. The nine thousand soldiers and refugees aboard had slept in her dining rooms and halls, crowded into the empty swimming pool, and stood up on deck. The *Cap Arcona* completed the evacuation, but at the expense of her turbines. They were completely worn out. Naval officials ordered her into dry dock in Copenhagen. Repairs returned her engines to service, but not to full strength. The *Cap Arcona*'s days of long-distance travel were over.

Decommissioning her, the navy returned her to her owners, Hamburg-Süd. Obergruppenführer-SS Karl Kaufmann, based in Lübeck, was in charge of what remained of the merchant marine. A short man with fine blond hair and a square face, he had just been appointed Commissioner for the Defense of Northern Germany and Reich Commissioner for Merchant Shipping. He ordered the *Cap Arcona* from Copenhagen Harbor to Neustadt Bay.

Also on March 30, Bernadotte visited Neuengamme concentration camp, just south of Hamburg, for the first time. Here he was to pick up his prisoners. Commanded by Sturmbannführer Max Pauly, a strong-jawed officer with a broad forehead and small, widely-spaced eyes, Neuengamme had become the collection point for prisoners evacuated from all the other camps. In essence, it was the last stop—and now, the largest camp in the Third Reich. Bernadotte found the Scandinavian prisoners—2,200 Danes and Norwegians from Sachsenhausen, 600 from Dachau, and 1,600 policemen from other camps—being held in a "better" part of the prison.

Bernadotte recalls, ". . . I thought, too, of the prisoners of whom I had caught a glimpse in a part of the camp where there were no Scandinavians, and where we had no power. There were thousands of unhappy human beings there. . . ."

Ahlhorn, just south of Bremen and 130 miles from Neustadt, was a primitive airfield, with simple barracks and rudimentary equipment. Nos. 193, 197, 263, and 609 Typhoon squadrons arrived here in early April. All four squadrons would play roles in the May 3 attack.

The motto of No. 193 was *aera et terram imperare*, "to command the air and earth." The squadron had received its first operational Typhoons in January 1943. No. 193 participated in the Normandy invasion, and then flew in Belgium. D. M. Taylor was Squadron Leader.

No. 197's motto was *findimus caelum* ("we cleave the sky"). Led by K. J. Harding, the group had also been flying Typhoons since January 1943. The squadron had helped soften up troop targets in France before D-day, and then flew in Belgium and the Netherlands. For the mission of May 3, No. 197 would temporarily relocate to Celle, 105 miles south of Neustadt Bay. Most of the pilots were experienced. In No. 197, for instance, fifty-seven of the seventy-five pilots would eventually qualify for the squadron's blue-and-red-striped tie, only awarded after a thousand combat hours.

One of the oldest RAF squadrons, No. 263, was formed in Italy during the First World War. Its motto was bold: *ex ungue leonem*—"by his claws [one knows] the lion." Receiving its first Typhoons in December 1943, the squadron flew close support for the Allied armies in France in the summer of 1944. Capt. Martin Rumbold was Squadron Leader.

No. 609, known as the "West Riding" squadron after its English home, had a fox-hunting cry—"Tally Ho!"—as its motto. It got its first Typhoons early, in April 1942. The squadron adopted rockets as its main armament in March 1944. It relocated to Normandy after D-day to provide air support, and then moved into the Netherlands. Its pilots also flew reconnaissance sweeps of Germany.

No. 609 had some colorful members. Johnny Baldwin, the Typhoon ace, had flown with the squadron. Flight Lieutenant Baron Jean de Selys Longchamps, a Belgian attached to No. 609, single-handedly took out Gestapo headquarters in Brussels on January 20, 1943. As he departed, he dropped Belgian and British flags. However, his attack was not authorized. Although he had killed some thirty Germans, he had also unwittingly blown the cover of a British spy on site. As a result, the Nazis were able to arrest numerous informants.

Squadron Leader L. W. F. "Pinkie" Stark earned a Distinguished Flying Cross in February 1944. He bailed out over France on July 1, when his plane was disabled by flak. With the help of the French Resistance he made his way back to England. A. G. H. "Lord" Billam and others in the squadron were instrumental in the attack on Walcheren Island, which eventually freed Antwerp.

Another significant squadron, No. 198, moved to Plantlünne, 177 miles southwest of Neustadt, at this time also. Its motto was *igni renatus* ("We are reborn by fire"). Founded in June 1918, then disbanded in September 1919, it was re-formed with Typhoons in December 1942. Johnny Baldwin came over from No. 609 to lead No. 198. The squadron moved to Normandy in July 1944, assisting in the breakout, then relocated to Belgium before arriving in Germany. Baldwin would be a key player on May 3.

On April 2 Bernadotte again met Himmler at Hohen-Lüchen. He persisted in his efforts to rescue as many prisoners as he could before the Nazis could exhaust or execute them. Having made an initial agreement, he now tried to improve on it. Eventually, he persuaded Himmler to allow him to take "all Danish and Norwegian women and the sick," in addition to prisoners already specified. The arrangement called for ". . . the dispatch to Sweden of all the Swedish and Norwegian women and all the invalids, together with a small proportion of the 461 Norwegian students in Neuengamme. . . . All of the Danish policemen were to be sent to Denmark. The Scandinavians sent to Sweden were not to be interned, but placed in hospitals or boarded out. . . . Himmler further agreed to the release of a certain number of interned Norwegian civilians . . . and some French citizens."

After the meeting, Bernadotte drove back to Berlin with General Walter Schellenberg, one of Himmler's closest aides. To the Swede's great surprise, Schellenberg inquired if Bernadotte would be willing to ask Eisenhower if he would discuss a "capitulation on the Western front"—essentially a German surrender to the Americans and British, but not to the Soviets. Himmler, he said, was concerned about the revenge the Soviets would take on German troops. He was also a virulent anti-Bolshevik. What Schellenberg did not mention was that Himmler, a clever strategist, also saw a way to drive a wedge between the Soviets and their Western allies. Astonished by Schellenberg's request, Bernadotte replied that Himmler himself would have to make such a dramatic overture.

Schellenberg also told Bernadotte "that Hitler had issued orders that the concentration camps at Buchenwald, Bergen-Belsen, and probably Theresienstadt as well should be evacuated and the prisoners compelled to cover a distance of about one hundred and ninety miles on foot." In other words, the Germans were not going to simply hand over their prisoners to the Allies when they arrived. "Schellenberg said that he had protested strongly against this order, and that after a stormy discussion he had succeeded in inducing Hitler to countermand it. The commandants of the camps had been instructed not to evacuate them, but to surrender the prisoners to the Allied troops. Similar instructions would be given in connection with Neuengamme."

Bernadotte realized that Germany was on the verge of collapse. He remarked on "the long lines of German refugees from East Prussia. . . . Silently the pitiable procession moved on, along roads lined with the carcasses of horses that had drawn the primitive vehicles used by the refugees until their strength gave out." Also, "German fighter planes and German anti-aircraft fire had almost ceased to exist during the last months of the war, and Allied airmen were able to attack all vehicles on the roads without interference."

Not only civilians, but also soldiers were in disarray: "German troops were retreating over the roads near Hamburg, at Neu-Brandenburg, and near other towns—small disorganized groups, almost without arms, almost as hopeless as the refugees from the east; soldiers who realized that the war was lost, that this was the end."

On April 4 the 1st Special Services Brigade entered Osnabrück to scant resistance. It was the largest German city the British had yet captured. The speed of their forward movement, while exhilarating, made it hard for air and ground forces to stay coordinated. As one officer wrote, "[T]he RAF had difficulty keeping tabs on the pace of the advance and yellow smoke had to be fired to keep enthusiastic Typhoons at bay."

On April 7, Gilel Storch, in Stockholm, made an urgent call to Dr. Felix Kersten, Himmler's personal physician and confidante. Storch had heard that Kaltenbrunner was planning to blow up Bergen-Belsen the next morning. He persuaded Kersten to telephone Dr. Rudolf Brandt, a key Himmler assistant, to intervene. When Himmler heard from Brandt, he countermanded the order. The incident was just one more example of the ongoing infighting between Himmler and Kaltenbrunner over the fate of concentration camp inmates.

On April 10, Schmidt marched me and my comrades out of the Dora-Mittelbau camp, where we had been pretending to assist with construction of the V-rockets. The British and Americans were closing in on Dora, just as the Soviets had on Auschwitz. Our second death march had begun.

A fellow prisoner in my group later gave this testimony about the experience:

> . . . Max Schmidt gave orders to evacuate the camp because the enemies were approaching. He told us to look at the barrels of his firearms if any of us would hit on the idea of escaping . . . The first day of our march was very dangerous and caused us many troubles. We marched from Blankenburg/Harz via Halberstadt to Magdeburg.
>
> The march route was about 65 kilometers [39 miles]. These 65 kilometers had to be done without any rest. Most of the prisoners wore very bad shoes or had none, and were also in very weak condition so that they could not walk properly. Also they got before they left the camp a hot meal, consisting of thick barley with pepper, salt, and onion, which was nearly uneatable. Nearly all of the prisoners swallowed this food greedily because they were starving. The result of this was that nearly all of them had diarrhea. For those men it was impossible to go on marching in the way they were ordered to. Those

who stopped on the road to relieve themselves from this complaint were shot at once.

After being shot, the prisoners' numbers were written down but were destroyed later. They were left where they were shot, and the march went on.

Very often prisoners attempted to adjust their shoes. To do this they had to sit on the ground. When SS-Rottenführer Dobrowolski (Rumanian nationality) passed by on a bicycle, he ordered them to continue. They begged permission to rest for a few minutes and so were shot. This was a regular occurrence.

Upon our arrival in Magdeburg, our guards ordered us onto several open barges. We floated down the Elbe toward Hamburg and the Baltic. There were only five hundred or so of us left. I remember this as a lovely journey, the only pleasant time in four years of captivity. We floated past pretty little farms, edging up to the river, completely "normal," with laundry hung out to dry, flower gardens, and neat yards. They reminded us of the years before the camps when we, too, had led "normal" lives. Drifting along, we made our way towards our ultimate destination—the Schmidt family farm in Neu Glassau.

5

A SPECIAL OPERATION

MAY 3, 1945. MORNING. I followed the other prisoners out of the *Cap Arcona's* Grand Salon and down a narrow, windowless corridor with a handrail. Here the air was close, but at least warm—a godsend after the cold march and boat ride. We clanged down a steep stairway, turning into another corridor. This passageway had rows of open doors. Looking in, I saw staterooms with beds, chairs, and tables. They were crowded with people dressed in striped prison clothing like ourselves. Fifteen to twenty or so prisoners shared rooms that were intended for two. But at least these people had rooms. Apparently there was no place for us here, for our guard took us down another stairway.

We descended deep into the ship, each deck appearing simpler and sparer than the one before. Finally, the sailor leading us stopped by a steel door with a bar across it. Lifting the bar, he directed us through. When the last man had entered, he clanged the door shut and dropped the bar.

We found ourselves in no stateroom. Instead, we were in a dank box about the size of a small modern-day basement. A single bulb hung from the ceiling. The bare walls and floor and some broken crates in the corner suggested a storeroom. We were not the first to arrive. In fact, so many other prisoners were already in the room, we could barely squeeze in. There wasn't space enough to sit down. There were no toilet facilities, just a foul, rusty bucket. There was no food and no water.

By any standard, it was a frightening place. The air was so close it was hard to breathe without gagging. It reeked with the odors of unwashed bodies, urine, and excrement. There was not a single window or porthole to see out of. I had never been in an atmosphere so oppressive and claustrophobic.

There were well over a hundred of us in that little room, yet strangely, the place was silent. The inmates seemed stunned. Talking to them, we found they were mainly from Neuengamme and Gross-Rosen, another camp near Hamburg. The inmates begged for food we didn't have. They told us they'd been locked in the storeroom for days.

On April 10—the same day we left Dora-Mittelbau—the evacuation of Neuengamme also began. As a British investigation put it,

> [O]n the advance of the Allied forces, arrangements were made to evacuate the [prisoners] in accordance with the order of the Reichsführer-SS [Himmler] that no prisoners were to fall into enemy hands.
>
> Immediately prior to the evacuation of the camp, its strength was approximately 13,500 in the camp itself, and 25,000 men and 10,300 women in the *Aussenkommandos* [satellite camps] administered by the camp.
>
> Prior to its evacuation, the camp was cleaned up as much as possible and all steps possible were taken to remove evidence of any kind of the malpractices which had been carried on.

The evacuation would peak during the week of April 20-27, when 6,800 prisoners were shipped to Lübeck by train.

On April 11, Allied troops liberated Dora-Mittelbau when Sgt.

Aurio Pierro of the U.S. 33rd Armored drove his tank right up to the gates without opposition. We had missed out once more—this time by just twenty-four hours.

On April 12, advance units of the U.S. 9th Army reached the Elbe. Eisenhower ordered them to halt. On April 13, people all over Germany—both free and imprisoned, and including us—heard that President Franklin Roosevelt had died the day before at his home in Warm Springs, Georgia. Of course the Nazis were overjoyed. However, Roosevelt's death did not in any way improve Germany's situation. Harry S. Truman was duly sworn in as president and the American war effort continued unabated.

On that day, as well, the 1st Special Services Brigade entered Hademstorg unopposed, followed closely by the 11th Armored, its tanks "fanning out on the flat German plain which spread due east as far as the Elbe."

Our own voyage down the Elbe, from Magdeburg towards Hamburg, did provide us with somewhat of a respite. However, we soon found that more hardship lay ahead.

As a fellow prisoner remembered, "[O]n this voyage several died from severe beating and were thrown overboard. The SS procured meat and other food and held parties. The SS were living in luxury whilst the prisoners were starving. A few died of hunger and thirst. Other prisoner[s] received water treated with Rivanol [an anti-bacterial agent]. Through this chemically prepared water, the diarrhea epidemic broke out again. They were beaten hard with cables because they panicked. A prisoner named Herman Joseph who was in charge of other prisoners took part in the beating of his fellow men. He was half-Jew himself and his civilian job was an architect." Ironically he was also the man whose vodka saved my life.

At Lauenberg our barges turned north onto the Elbe-Lübeck Canal. At Bad Schwartau, just outside Lübeck, we disembarked, dividing into several groups. Our group of a hundred or so marched inland eighteen miles, arriving at the Schmidt family farm in the little village of Neu Glassau on April 14.

A fellow prisoner recalled:

> On this march more prisoners were shot. On arrival at
> Siblin [Neu Glassau][we] were put in a shed of the
> farmer [Schmidt]. Next day the aforementioned Max
> Schmidt came to count the prisoners. When he discov-
> ered too many prisoners still alive, he stopped the issue
> of cigarettes and alcohol to the SS troops. Max Schmidt
> told his men that if more of the prisoners had been shot,
> they would have [gotten] more rations. This will give
> you a picture of what type of man he was.
>
> The following day the prisoners received very bad
> food: raw carrots, which generally are used for feeding
> cattle, were put into boiling water and given to the pris-
> oners. This was the usual hot meal. In addition they got
> one loaf of bread for ten men and 10–20 gram[s] mar-
> garine. This was given twice a week.

Why had Schmidt brought us to his family's farm? With the closing of Neuengamme there was no camp left to take us to. Also, if
Schmidt had us to guard, no one could send him to the eastern
front, where almost certain death awaited. The Soviets were
slaughtering German troops by the thousands as they advanced. As
long as Schmidt had us to brutalize, he had a job that kept him out
of harm's way.

On April 14, the same day we reached Schmidt's farm, the *Cap Arcona* arrived in Germany from Denmark, picking up a mooring in
Neustadt Bay. She found another converted passenger ship already
there, also sent by Kaufmann, also built by Blohm & Voss, also a vet-
eran of the Gdynia-Copenhagen runs. Displacing 21,056 tons, the
Deutschland was over 450 feet long and 65 feet abeam, with two funnels, four cargo masts, a clipper stern, twin propellers, and a service
speed of 16 knots. Owned by the Hamburg-Amerika Line, a Hamburg-Süd rival, she had a normal carrying capacity of 420 crew and
1,558 passengers—221 in first class, 402 in second, and 935 in third.

Since her launching on April 28, 1923, the *Deutschland* had traveled between Hamburg, Southampton, and New York. After the navy commandeered her in 1939, she had served as floating accommodations in Gdynia, like the *Cap Arcona*, and, later, as evacuation transport. On seven trips to and from Copenhagen between January and April, 1945, the *Deutschland* had carried 70,000 refugees.

The bay in which the two ships were moored was named for the straightforward, no-nonsense town of Neustadt ("New City") on its southern rim. Windowless brick warehouses and tall concrete silos loomed over a working waterfront. A canal led inland to a small harbor and the town center. At the mouth of this waterway lay a U-boat school, which consisted of a dozen or so wooden barracks for the cadets, a running track, a playing field with a grandstand, and a gymnasium. A marine garrison protected and operated the school.

In 1945 the population of Neustadt was approximately 20,000. The town square boasted several three-story municipal and commercial buildings, including a town hall and a bank built of brick and stucco. The spire of the Gothic church was the tallest structure, soaring some thirty feet above the rooftops of the other buildings. Rows of slim poplars lined the waterfront.

The low-lying shores to the east and west of the town were dotted with two-story frame houses fronting on narrow sandy beaches. Saw grass, shrubs, and wind-stunted trees grew here. From Rettin in the west to Travemünde in the east, the full shoreline of Neustadt Bay stretched some eighteen miles.

Also on April 14, Himmler made his infamous reply to a joint query from the commandants of the Dachau and Flossenburg concentration camps. They had requested permission to hand over their populations to the Allies when they arrived, rather than execute the inmates, as Kaltenbrunner had ordered them to do under Hitler's March 19 "Destructive Measures on Reich Territory" decree. However, on April 14 Himmler "[instructed the commandants] on no account to surrender their camps to the enemy, but evacuate them immediately." His exact wording was: "Handing-over [to the Allies] is quite out of the question. The camp is to be evacuated immediately. 'No prisoner is to fall into enemy hands alive.' "

The narrator of the 1995 film, *Der Fall* Cap Arcona (*The Case of the* Cap Arcona), claims Himmler sent the message to "all camp commandants." If so, he went against a promise he had made to Kersten, not to pass on Hitler's order of destruction.

Historian Roy C. Nesbit holds that "by inference [Himmler's order] meant that either [the prisoners] were to be moved back from the Allied lines of advance or they were to be killed. Both alternatives took place with the victims of Neuengamme."

The question of what to do with the prisoners had reached a crisis point. The actual reason the commandant of Dachau wanted to hand over his prisoners was because inmates were dying faster than his prisoner work crews could drag them out of the camp and bury them, and he had also run out of the coal he needed to fuel his crematoria.

According to a Nazi official named Gerdes, an administrative functionary who testified at Kaltenbrunner's trial at Nuremberg, a grim remedy was now suggested: "[I]n the middle of April, 1945 [one] Gauleiter Giesler disclosed the fact to me that Obergruppenführer Kaltenbrunner had given him instructions, in accordance with an order from the Führer, that there should be made an immediate plan regarding the liquidation of the concentration camp at Dachau and the two Jewish work camps at Mühldorf and Landsberg. The instructions stated that the two Jewish work camps at Landsberg and Mühldorf were to be destroyed by the German Air Force, since the sites of these two camps had lately and repeatedly been affected by hostile bombing attacks. The action was given the camouflage name, 'Cloud A-1.' "

When the Luftwaffe balked, Hitler's aide suggested an alternative: "For the concentration camp Dachau, Kaltenbrunner [then] ordered the action 'Cloud Fire' which stipulated that the inmates of the concentration camps at Dachau, with the exception of the Aryan members of the Western Powers, were to be liquidated with poison.

"Gauleiter Giesler received that order directly from Kaltenbrunner and in my presence he discussed with the Health Officer, Dr. Harfeld, the procurement of the necessary amount of poison."

The only alternative to mass murder, given that "no prisoner [was] to fall into enemy hands alive," was seen to be evacuation of the camps. But where were camp commandants to send their prisoners? The only still unthreatened part of Germany left was the rural province of Schleswig-Holstein. The Jutland Peninsula lay just beyond, but that was primarily Danish and the Danes hated the Nazis, who had been occupying their country since 1940. The Danes had also actively helped Jews. In fact, they had transported a thousand Jews to safety in Sweden one night. Even if the Germans could get their prisoners to Denmark, by rail or road, it was hardly an ideal site.

Still, the commandants had their orders. So they evacuated their camps, driving their captives north and west on death marches to other camps, many of which were too crowded to accept new inmates. In these cases, the Nazis simply murdered their prisoners.

At Bergen-Belsen guards ordered one large group of prisoners out of their railway cars when the camp would not take them. They marched the inmates to the nearby village of Gardelegen. There Gauleiter Gerhard Thiele ordered the 1,038 men and boys into a large brick barn. SS troops had already poured gasoline and oil on the straw inside. Just before guards slid shut—and locked—the second of two huge doors, Scharführer-SS Erhart Brauny threw a burning torch into the building. SS troops, Luftwaffe soldiers, and *Volksturm* (People's Militia) fired on prisoners who tried to escape. Some managed to dig under the walls, but they were shot as they emerged. One thousand and sixteen people died; only twenty-two somehow escaped.

On April 15 the British 2nd Army overpowered light German resistance and liberated Bergen-Belsen. They found 10,000 unburied corpses and 40,000 sick and dying prisoners. These were the ones who hadn't already been murdered or evacuated. During the following weeks, another 28,000 died, too far gone to take food or recover. There were heaps of emaciated corpses, so many that the British had to use bulldozers to bury them to prevent outbreaks of disease. Anne Frank had died at the camp just a few weeks earlier.

On April 16, the British Chiefs of Staff "formally declared the end of area bombing." At the same time, apparently in response to the widespread criticism of the Dresden raid and "Bomber" Harris's unrepentant reaction, Churchill made a dramatic change in the responsibilities of his three air force commands. He transferred responsibility for German skies from Bomber Command to Fighter Command, and for coastal airspace from Bomber Command to Coastal Command. This decision would have implications.

In fact, Struan Robertson at the University of Hamburg believes this change had a direct effect on the May 3 tragedy. "Winston Churchill had given [this] order following the bombing of Dresden which he had criticized as a willful act of terror and destruction. This decision replacing Bomber Command with Fighter Command had serious consequences that resulted in the bombing of the prison ships [on May 3]. Bomber Command's aerial reconnaissance was best informed regarding events and changes on the ground in Germany. They knew the exact position of concentration camps and so where not to bomb. For example, not one bomb landed on Neuengamme concentration camp near Hamburg. In fact, planes had flown low over the camp, waggling their wings, giving hope to the prisoners on the parade ground. Headquarters of [Fighter Command's] Second Tactical Air Arm in Süchteln had little knowledge of the transport of concentration camp prisoners northwards." While it turns out that the change in responsibilities was not, in fact, the direct cause of the disaster, inasmuch as the change compromised the quality of intelligence, it certainly contributed.

The night of April 16, the Soviet submarine L-3 sank the passenger ship SS *Goya*, sending 6,200 more German refugees and soldiers to their deaths.

On April 17, Kaufmann ordered a third ship to take on prisoners in Neustadt Bay. The *Thielbek* was a 273-foot freighter with a displacement of 2,815 tons. Having been badly bombed the summer before, she was undergoing repairs at the Maschinenbau-Gesellschaft shipyard in Lübeck. At the confluence of the Wakenitz and the Trave rivers, Lübeck was a major seaport and Germany's largest harbor on the Baltic. The city had a population of 230,000 in 1945. The great width and depth of the Trave River enabled the port to handle vessels of considerable size, and the city was famous for her yards and facilities. The *Thielbek's* steering gear was inoperable, and she was waiting for new electric motors for her rudder. Suddenly, Kaufmann ordered tugboats to tow her out of the yard to a pier across the harbor. Kaufmann advised her captain, Johann Jacobsen, to prepare for "a special operation." Outfitted with a single funnel and two cargo masts, the *Thielbek* was not a passenger ship, but a freighter. She had two holds fore and aft, but accommodations for just a small crew.

On April 17, Bernadotte wrote to Gilel Storch in Stockholm. "Today I can announce that 423 Jews are expected to arrive tomorrow in Sweden, where they are to remain until the end of the war. According to information provided by the Swedish Red Cross delegate who picked them up at Theresienstadt, these 423 individuals comprise all of the Scandinavian Jews who were in Theresienstadt and nearby camps." This was a small ray of hope for all Jews in concentration camps. However, as Josek and I were to find out, it was very small indeed.

Bernadotte had by this time set up a Swedish Red Cross mission in Lübeck to process the prisoners in his care. Major Dr. Hans Arnoldson, a close friend, was its head. The International Red Cross from Geneva also had a presence in the city. One P. [first name unknown] de Blonay was in charge. He would play a crucial role in trying to prevent the May 3 disaster.

On April 18, SS troopers made unannounced visits to Captain Bertram on the *Cap Arcona* and Captain Jacobsen on the *Thielbek*,"inviting" them to a conference ashore.

At the meeting, which Gauleiter Kaufmann himself may or may not have attended, SS officials explained that the Third Reich had run out of locations to keep its prisoners on land. Kaufmann had therefore decided to put them on ships. The captains should prepare to take large numbers of concentration camp prisoners on board. There could be as many as ten thousand prisoners, primarily from Neuengamme. A small freighter, the *Athen*, would ferry the inmates out to the *Cap Arcona* and *Thielbek*.

The *Cap Arcona* was designed to carry a total of 1,945 crew and passengers. Captain Jacobsen's *Thielbek* was not meant to carry any passengers.

Both captains protested. They were professional sailors, devoted to their ships and crews. Captain Bertram later wrote in his official report to his employer, the Hamburg-Süd, "For me it was matter of course to refuse to accept the prisoners, since any responsible seaman knows that the risk at sea to take on human beings without absolute necessity during wartime is dangerous enough, especially such masses." Captain Jacobsen, sixty years old, a career seafarer, returned to the *Thielbek* feeling depressed and powerless.

In the meantime, Max Pauly continued to evacuate Neuengamme. Guards loaded the prisoners into open cattle cars, fifty to a car, twenty cars to a train. Eventually, Pauly would send fourteen thousand prisoners to Lübeck to be loaded onto ships. Of these, four thousand would die on the way.

The night of April 18, Bernadotte, back at Schloss Friedrichsruh near Lübeck, learned that the evacuation of Neuengamme would be completed the next day. "The reason for the evacuation of the entire camp . . . was the publicity that the Allies had given to the conditions in the concentration camps at Buchenwald and Bergen-Belsen— though Himmler insisted that the publicity was a tissue of lies."

Accordingly, reported Bernadotte, "The very next day we started removing all the Scandinavians from Neuengamme. . . . The non-Scandinavians were pushed into freight trains whose destination no one knew. Questioned about it, the German commandant [Pauly] shrugged his shoulders: '*Keine Ahnung*' ('I have no idea'). Of course, he was lying."

That same day, April 19, the first Neuengamme prisoners arrived by train in Lübeck. They were marched to Neustadt, twelve miles north. Here, they were separated into two groups. The fortunate ones went with Bernadotte, boarding one of two white hospital ships, the *Magdalena* or *Lillie-Matthiessen*, lying in Neustadt Bay. The others went to the *Cap Arcona* and *Thielbek*. Either Arnoldson or de Blonay, or the two together, managed to redirect another 250 to 300 from this group to Bernadotte, no doubt saving their lives.

6

THIS INSANE ORDER

APRIL 27, 1945. LATE AFTERNOON. THE SCHMIDT FARM, NEU GLASSAU.
My brother and I almost escaped the *Cap Arcona* entirely. Just a few
days before we boarded, we came very close to being liberated. We
nearly saw the end of four years of misery, deprivation, beatings,
cold, and starvation. Ironically, the opportunity came on a beach
on Neustadt Bay close to the one from which we eventually em-
barked for the *Cap Arcona*.

Also ironically, the opportunity came through Max Schmidt, my
jailer and oppressor, the murderer of many prisoners. He had
saved my life once before—with the timely offer of Hermann's
vodka—and now, he would try again.

We'd been at the Schmidt farm for about two weeks. We slept
on straw in the huge brick barn, but the food was better than any
we'd had in the camps, and we didn't have to work. One afternoon, I was standing outside the barn, alone, when Max Schmidt
came up to me. Quietly he said, "The Vice-Chairman of the
Swedish Red Cross, Count Folke Bernadotte, will be here tomorrow to take some prisoners to Sweden. It's a mercy mission. However, he's let it be known that he'll only take prisoners from
Western Europe. No Poles, Slavs, or Czechs."

I listened carefully. Why was he telling me this?

"On the other hand," he continued, "he won't know where any of you are from. And I don't have any records. So—if you want to tell him you're from the West, you can. I won't betray you."

I considered. What were the risks? The alternatives? Would I go from the proverbial frying pan into the fire? I asked, "What happens if I just stay here, with everyone else?"

He shook his head. "I can't tell you. No one can. The Commandant of Neuengamme, Max Pauly, is in charge of all the prisoners in the area now. I know him, and I don't trust him." He paused. "What I'm saying is, the farther you are from here, the safer you are."

"Thank you," I said, "for the opportunity." He nodded and walked off.

I went straight to my brother, Josek, and drew him out of the group he was standing with. I was completely astounded by what Schmidt had told me. There was a chance we could escape. And not only wouldn't Schmidt stand in my way—he had been the one to reveal it to me! When I told Josek, he was equally amazed. We talked for a long time about whether to take the risk of being found out, and what it would mean if we succeeded. Being discovered didn't seem much of a risk. After all, Schmidt himself had suggested the plan. He wouldn't punish us. And what would the Swedes do, other than give us a reprimand? Truly, what could be worse than the camps we had already been to?

If we succeeded, we would be free—and alive. We would end up in Sweden. The only drawback was, we couldn't return to Poland—our native land and our family's home. That was a hard thing to think about. But eventually we came to the conclusion that we no longer needed to consider Poland our home. After all, everyone in our family was dead. We also knew we'd continue to face anti-Semitism if we moved back. Yes, we would have to give up all hope of returning to Dobra. On the other hand, from what Schmidt had implied about Pauly, our best chance for survival lay in trying to bluff our way to freedom tomorrow. We also agreed not to tell anyone else; so many would want to try that no one would be able to escape.

I picked France as our country—a bit of a challenge, because although I spoke fluent German, I had just a little French. Josek spoke none. Immediately I began to tutor him in the simple phrases and everyday words that I could remember. We would have to hope that the Swedes wouldn't know much French, either.

Sturmbannführer-SS Christoph-Heinz Gehrig, administrative head of Neuengamme, now arrived in Lübeck to supervise the loading of prisoners. Most of them were Jewish or Eastern European. Among other horrors, Gehrig had been responsible for the murder of twenty Jewish children in a Hamburg school, after using them as subjects in tuberculosis experiments at Neuengamme.

Prisoner Philip Jackson remembers leaving Neuengamme with his father:

> We (my father and myself) with a few hundred other prisoners, including the hospital sick, left Neuengamme by train, passed through Hamburg and arrived in Lübeck [in] the afternoon. . . . Our train stopped at the quayside.
>
> The following boats were alongside the quay in Lübeck—SS *Athen*, SS *Thielbek*, and SS *Elmenhorst*. These three ships were then loaded with prisoners from other trainloads and our own.
>
> We remained ten days in Lübeck in the train tending the sick, such as we were able. The sick in the *waggons* [cattle cars] were in a terrible condition—they were starved and could not move, and performed their acts of nature on the floor of the wagon if they could not move to the barrel provided for that purpose. It must be remembered that there was overcrowding and the stench was unbelievable.

When Gehrig's troops ordered the first prisoners onto the *Thielbek*, the ship was still dockside in Lübeck. Representatives of the Swedish Red Cross were present as monitors. However, the ship was German and it was not a hospital ship; there was a limit to what they felt they could do on behalf of the prisoners. The Nazis gave packets of food to all of the inmates except the Russians. Because of malnutrition and dehydration, for many prisoners consumption of this food led to terrible and unanticipated suffering rather than renewed health.

Using leather whips, kapos drove the prisoners down ladders into the cargo holds until First Officer Andresen finally ordered them to stop.

Second Officer Walter Felgner later described the scene: "About 1,200 to 1,500 prisoners arrived that first day . . . The next morning, we pulled the [dead] bodies of twenty or thirty prisoners out of [the holds]. This was repeated every day. If you could have seen what it looked like . . . It was appalling. They all stood. They couldn't lie down. . . . They used buckets as toilets, which were emptied every day and invariably slopped about." There was very little drinking water. The stench of humanity, sweat, and excrement was overpowering.

Interviewed for the film *Typhoons' Last Storm*, prisoner Pierre Billaux remembers dead bodies being hauled out of the holds on ropes attached to hands, legs, necks—anything that could be got hold of. They would "swing from left to right, in and out of the shaft of light" shining down from the open hatch above. The SS eventually crowded 2,800 prisoners onto the *Thielbek*.

The next morning, April 20, Gehrig ordered Fritz Nobmann, captain of the freighter *Athen*, to ferry 280 guards and 2,300 prisoners out to the *Cap Arcona*. The *Athen* had her own berth in Neustadt. Built in 1936, she displaced 4,451 tons, making her somewhat larger than the *Thielbek*. She had a single funnel on her wheelhouse and cargo holds fore and aft.

Nobmann refused Gehrig's order. Gehrig responded by threatening him with summary court-martial and execution on the spot. Nobmann capitulated. Guards drove prisoners onto the *Athen* using fists, boots, and whips. They forced them onto rope ladders leading down into the holds. The prisoners fell all over themselves. Many were seriously injured.

The prisoner Mikelis Mezmalietis clearly remembers his time on the *Athen:* "There were carefully arranged piles of goods on the deck, covered with tarpaulin. There were two holds for the cargo in the ship, both with floors made of metal plates. I was taken to the second, the one deepest down, closest to the ships [sic] hull. In the floor of the hold there were round holes about 14 inches in diameter. We used these as latrines, since nothing else had been provided, either in our hold or the one above us."

As the *Athen* drew alongside the *Cap Arcona*, Captain Bertram was waiting on deck. He refused to allow the prisoners to be put aboard, even after SS troops came onto his ship and threatened him. He "[gave] as his reasons for this action that the ship had no means of defending itself and that he considered it unsafe for thousands of people to be placed on a ship and thereby exposed to the dangers of air attacks, U-boat attacks, and mines." In addition, he said, "all lifebelts, except [those] sufficient for the crew, had been handed in."

The *Athen* pulled away, then headed out into the bay to "throw overboard persons who had died on the ship." When she returned, she moored a short distance away from the *Cap Arcona* for the night. The prisoners on board were given nothing to drink or eat.

The next morning, April 21, the *Athen* returned to her berth at Neustadt, having failed to unload her cargo of inmates. When Gehrig heard about Bertram's refusal, he notified Pauly. Pauly in turn contacted Count Bassewitz-Behr, Chief of Gestapo in Hamburg, who reported to Kaufmann. That evening, Kaufmann sent his personal adviser, one Hauptsturmführer-SS Horn, to the Chairman of the Board of Hamburg-Süd, John Eggert. Horn told Eggert that Bertram was to take the prisoners aboard or be shot. Furthermore, Kaufmann would impound the *Cap Arcona*.

Eggert called Bertram to tell him of this ultimatum. Bertram in turn telephoned Admiral Engelhardt, Chief of Naval Transport. The Admiral sent a representative to Kaufmann to lodge a formal protest, but the man never got to the commissioner. Intercepting him, Horn dismissed the protest himself, and then informed Gehrig. All of this took several days.

Bernadotte met once again with Himmler on April 21. The Reichsführer had just come from a meeting with Norbert Masur of the World Jewish Congress, arranged by Kersten. Himmler had promised that no more Jews would be killed, the camps would be handed over to the Allies, and any Jewish women in Ravensbrück would be evacuated—as long as they were not identified as Poles. When Bernadotte asked to be "allowed to remove all French-women interned at the Ravensbrück concentration camp, Himmler . . . not only assented to this, but [said] that he also wished us to remove the women of all nationalities. . . ."

The next day, April 22, according to one account, "2,873 women—of Polish, French, Belgian, and Dutch origins, as well as 1,607 Jews—were evacuated [by the Swedish Red Cross] from Ravensbrück."

However, the transfer did not occur without interference. Hauptsturmführer-SS Fritz Suhren, commandant of the camp, initially refused to release the women. He said "he had explicit Führer orders to liquidate the women upon the approach of enemy troops." Nonetheless, and most fortunately, the Swedish representatives managed to prevail.

On the night of April 23, Bernadotte and Himmler met yet again, this time at the Swedish Embassy in Lübeck. By now, Himmler had moved his own headquarters to Lübeck. Convening at 11:00 P.M., they had to take to the cellar during an air raid which cut off power—and conversation. When they resumed their discussion over candles, Himmler asked Bernadotte to take a request from him to Eisenhower via the Swedish government. He was willing to offer Eisenhower, on his own authority alone, the surrender of all German forces on the Western front. Himmler had come to the conclusion that Hitler was going to stay in Berlin rather than move to a more secure location, and would refuse to the very end to make terms with the Allies. Bernadotte agreed, with conditions. One of them was that he be allowed to evacuate all of the Scandinavian prisoners, male and female, at Neuengamme. Himmler consented.

Bernadotte then asked Himmler to put his offer down on paper. He promised to see the note got to Günther in Stockholm. The Foreign Minister would forward the message to Eisenhower. As Bernadotte wrote later, "Himmler immediately did as requested.

He also declared that, if a meeting could be arranged between himself and Eisenhower, he was willing to make roughly the following declaration: 'I recognize that German arms have suffered defeat at the hands of the Western powers. I am prepared to surrender unconditionally on the Western front, and also to discuss the technical ways and means of arranging the capitulation of the German armed forces in Denmark and Norway."

On April 24, Captain Jacobsen wrote a letter to his wife describing conditions aboard the *Thielbek*: "The dead are removed from the [holds] every morning. We had five this morning. But because [the number of corpses] increases so rapidly, they are being picked up [by boats, to be taken ashore] . . . prisoners of all ages from 14 to 70 and from ministers, professors, doctors, captains, to workers—all are represented. Germans, Hungarians, Poles, French, etc. represent the nationalities. The foreigners are forced to go and remain in the [holds]; they are not allowed on deck. They are crammed in like sardines."

On April 25, "at 4:40 in the afternoon, near Torgau, on the river Elbe, a First Lieutenant and three men of a United States Intelligence and Reconnaissance Platoon found themselves face to face with men of the Red Army." East and West had finally met. The individuals immediately returned to their respective headquarters and informed their superiors.

The next morning, April 26, Gehrig, accompanied by two other officers and two soldiers armed with machine guns, accosted Captain Bertram on the waterfront in Neustadt. As Bertram later described it, "Gehrig had brought a written order to my attention for me to be shot at once if I would further refuse to take the prisoners on board. At this point it became clear to me that even my death would not prevent boarding of the prisoners, and so I informed the SS officer that I categorically declined any responsibility for my ship."

In fact, reported Thure Dommenget, Bertram's Second Officer—who was with him at the time—the captain also told Gehrig, "I have a wife and two children. That is the only reason why I will comply with this insane order."

Bertram reported, "Gehrig proceeded to order the transfer of the prisoners from the *Athen* to the *Cap Arcona* [and so the loading began]. Additional transports arrived from Lübeck, so that [eventually], I had a total of about 6,500 prisoners on board."

According to Struan Robertson, before the *Athen* ferried the first prisoners out to the *Cap Arcona*, SS troopers under one Untersturmführer Kirstein had gone aboard. Gathering up all the life jackets set aside for passengers, they locked them in a storage room, together with all the wooden benches they could find. They set aside flotation devices for only the crew and themselves. Then they smashed holes in all but a few of the lifeboats.

Dommenget said later, "[T]he rumor got about that the entire ship, together with the crew and prisoners, was to be sunk. To pretend it [the Holocaust] had never happened. Who knows whether it [the rumor] was true? But it certainly looked that way."

Historian Roy C. Nesbit says, "Some of the seamen on the *Cap Arcona* were told that the prisoners were to be taken out to sea and then collected by Swedish Red Cross ships, but this assurance was probably a means of allaying their fears."

Of course, such a plan was impossible. Bernadotte had brought only two ships, and the space on them had already been allocated to several thousand Scandinavian inmates. The ships could have taken just a small fraction of the over seven thousand prisoners on the *Cap Arcona*, *Thielbek*, and *Athen*.

Nesbit continues, "It is probable that the SS simply regarded the ships as convenient prisons where the inmates of Neuengamme could be kept under guard either to rot or be killed by the RAF; they were obeying Himmler's orders to the last."

SS guards settled themselves into the luxury suites on the upper decks of the *Cap Arcona*. About fifty women joined them—East Prussian relatives, female troops, and girlfriends. Two hundred *Volksturm*—older men serving as home guards—arrived to augment the SS.

Accommodations for prisoners depended on where they were from. The SS put German inmates in first-class cabins, although they crowded them in. They assigned Poles and Czechs second-class rooms. Western Europeans (French, Italian, and Dutch) rated third-class accommodations. The SS shut the Russians in the cargo holds in the bow originally used to carry bananas, automobiles, and other freight back from South America. Conditions here were atrocious. Most of the other prisoners at least had fresh air, a view of the world outside, and access to water and plumbing.

Franz Wolff, ship's boy on the *Cap Arcona* at the time, remembers the loading: "[When] the people started coming aboard, [they were] horrific people. They were all *muselmanen*, so terribly skinny. The old sailors covered my eyes so I couldn't see it . . . The captain of the *Athen* said, 'This is the worst scandal in history.' The crew had never seen anything as terrible as these concentration camp prisoners."

The crews were appalled not only by the condition of the prisoners, but also by the brutality of the SS. As one historian puts it, "Relations between [the] guards [on the *Cap Arcona* and *Thielbek*] and the ships' crews approached open hostility, for the seamen were loath to accept responsibility for the prisoners when the Allies eventually reached them, but these crews were powerless against the guns and superior numbers of the SS."

The Nazis had turned the ships into floating concentration camps. Furthermore, it was the impression of both crew and prisoners on the *Cap Arcona* that instead of using crematoria to eliminate their enemies, the Nazi had simply decided to use the ships. They would scuttle the vessels, drowning the prisoners en masse. Everyone knew it was only a matter of days before the British and Americans would arrive.

There were no indications from the exteriors of the ships that the *Cap Arcona* and *Thielbek* actually held concentration camp prisoners.

"No attempt was made to paint either ship white, nor were Red Cross insignia displayed," explains air historian Roy C. Nesbit. "It is known that Bertram tried to obtain permission to light up his ship at night, but this was refused." The crew of the nearby *Deutschland* did manage to paint one large red cross on the ship's after funnel before running out of paint.

On April 26, President Truman's reply to Himmler's offer, made after consulting Churchill and informing Stalin, arrived in

Stockholm. The first sentence made the Allied position clear: " 'A German offer of surrender will be accepted only if it be complete on all fronts, as regards Great Britain and the Soviet Union as well as the United States.' " In other words, there would be no separate peace. The fighting—and the suffering—would continue.

At four o'clock that afternoon, twenty-four hours after the first contact between U.S. and Soviet troops, "divisional commanders, the Commander of the [U.S.] 69th Division, and the Commander of the Russian 58th Guards Division, met in Torgau."

Historian Clay Blair explains what was really going on: "In a little-known operation [U.S. elements] crossed the Elbe River . . . 'linked up' with the Red Army and blocked it from moving farther northwest to Lübeck and Kiel. . . ." This was key to protecting Denmark from Russian occupation, an important concern of the British. As Churchill had said, "There is no reason why the Russians should occupy Denmark, which is a country to be liberated and to have its sovereignty restored."

Photographs of the soldiers show them shaking hands and hugging. They share bottles of wine and big smiles. American privates dance outdoors with Russian secretaries under large, framed pictures of Roosevelt and Stalin hung on trees.

On April 27, in Odense, Denmark, Bernadotte informed Schellenberg of the Allied response to Himmler's offer. On April 28, word of Himmler's attempted capitulation was leaked to the Reuters news agency, which broadcast the story worldwide. Hitler immediately ordered Himmler's arrest. He also appointed Admiral Karl Dönitz his successor as President of the Reich and Supreme Commander of the Armed Forces. Until then, Himmler had been his choice. Dönitz had risen to prominence as Chief of U-boats, experiencing dramatic successes in the early days of the war that had won him Hitler's attention and approbation. Sharp-chinned, clear-eyed, and intelligent, Dönitz managed to convince the members of the Nuremberg tribunal at the end of the war that he had no knowledge of concentration camp atrocities.

The Nazi command structure was crumbling. A British commando wrote of this time, "The war against Germany was almost over. The British Army had overcome all obstacles, and before them lay a clear road to the Baltic. Soon the Elbe would be bridged, and the tanks crossing, to stream in long columns across Schleswig-Holstein."

In fact, at two o'clock on the morning of April 29, the 1st Special Services Brigade did cross the Elbe in amphibious Buffaloes. They captured the town of Lauenburg, on the opposite side, at dawn. The British were now just forty-six miles from Neustadt.

That same morning, Captain Bertram made a special trip to Hamburg. In a postwar report to his employer, Hamburg-Süd, he explained that he went "to request release from the order to scuttle the ship in case the enemy approached." Officials in Hamburg assured him that his request was irrelevant. There would be no scuttling. Oberstgruppenführer Abraham, chief of staff to Bassewitz-Behr, told Bertram that Bernadotte had "just declared he would take over all prisoners except German nationals, and [Bertram] should speedily return to Neustadt."

Abraham was lying. Bernadotte had made no such declaration. He had no such permission—or capacity of transport. While Bertram never identified the origin of the order to scuttle his ship, it is clear he believed there was a plan was to sink the *Cap Arcona* with all aboard. Otherwise, why would he have made the long trip to Hamburg? While there are no records of what questions the captains of the *Athen* and *Thielbek* might have had, there seems little reason to believe that the plans for these ships and their occupants were any different. As for scuttling, Neustadt was, of course, home to a U-boat school. There were many armed submarines in the harbor.

On April 29, American forces liberated Dachau. Pauly completed the evacuation of Neuengamme.

The next day, Hitler committed suicide in his bunker.

Tanks of the 11th Armored crossed the Elbe at Lauenburg and headed for the Baltic, with 1st Special Services Brigade, which had led it over, now behind, "moving east in [its] wake, clearing villages and small towns which might hold pockets of enemy troops. . . ."

That same day, according to Bertram's report, "the *Athen* took [away] 2,000 German prisoners on board so that at the time of the sinking of the *Cap Arcona*, only about 4,500 prisoners were on board." A clerk on board the ship put the figure at 5,500.

On May 1, Dönitz announced Hitler's death in a radio address to the nation. He also "urged the continuation of the struggle: 'I take over the supreme command of all branches of the armed forces with the intention of carrying on the war. . . .' "

In the evening Dönitz met with Himmler at his headquarters in Plön, twenty-four miles northwest of Lübeck. He did not arrest Himmler, as he had been ordered to do, most probably because he needed Himmler's networks of secret police and intelligence personnel in order to continue to mount some sort of resistance to the Allied advance. He also denied the Gauleiter of Hamburg permission to surrender the city to the Allies.

Dönitz intended to continue fighting. It was no accident that he was in Schleswig-Holstein, rather than Berlin. The Scandinavian countries were nearby. The Nazis still held Norway. As Bernadotte, who was on the scene, notes, Dönitz and the military commanders close to him "were not at that time in any circumstances prepared to give up Norway without a fight. They particularly pointed out that the German commander in Norway, Colonel General Böhme, was in a very strong strategic position."

7

I Saw So Many Dead

APRIL 28, 1945. EARLY MORNING. As Schmidt cracked open the barn doors the morning the Swedish Red Cross was due at the farm, Josek and I were up out of the straw and onto our feet in a flash.

A long black limousine was the first glimpse we had of the Swedish mission. A Red Cross flag fluttered from its left fender as it came slowly up the dirt road to the farm. Four white troop trucks followed, each with huge red crosses on their canvas covers. The entourage stopped in front of the barn. The drivers switched off their engines. Out of the limousine stepped three men, wearing pressed khaki uniforms. They were tall, blue-eyed, and blond-haired. They also looked well fed. One carried an elegant baton under his arm. I assumed—but don't know for sure—that he was Count Bernadotte.

Schmidt ordered us into our customary formation. The man with the baton called in German, "All Western nationals, step forward!"

This was the moment. Maybe fifty prisoners stepped out of line. I knew most of them. They were mainly from France, Holland, and Belgium. There had been some Norwegians with us, but they were all dead. There were no Americans or British. I tugged at Josek's jacket. We walked forward and stood with the others. Seeing us do this, some other Eastern Europeans stepped up.

I held my breath, but no one objected. Not the man I assumed
was Bernadotte, not the other two Swedish officers, not Schmidt.
We simply formed up and marched to the trucks.

My heart was pounding with excitement. It was hard to believe
all this was really happening. But the truck drivers rolled up the
canvas flaps at the back of their vehicles, unlatched and dropped
the tailgates, and urged us in. Afraid that someone would order us
back, Josek and I made sure to be among the first to load. I cannot
describe the feeling of climbing into that truck. Josek and I looked
at each other to be sure that what we were living through was not
a dream. We were on our way to freedom and life. We were saying goodbye forever to terror, deprivation, shame, and want.

The trucks started up. Turning around in the barnyard, they
followed the limousine back down the dirt road. I couldn't see
much from the truck, just a final view of the barn out the back.
Glimpses of blue sky and treetops bounced into view as I headed
off to my new life.

After half an hour or so of driving on winding country roads, we
pulled off to one side, descended a gentle pitch, and rolled to a
stop. When we got out, we were on a beach. Low dunes stretched
away on either side. Before us lay a huge body of water. I couldn't
see the end of it. It was Neustadt Bay, I discovered later, with
Lübeck Bay beyond. A few small trees and some clumps of grass
were the only vegetation. About a mile offshore, a white ship—a
hospital ship—rode at anchor, a flag flapping from its bridge in the
stiff breeze. The flag was pale blue with a thin yellow cross—
Swedish. Dinghies from the ship advanced across the water.

Once again the man with the baton called for our attention. Fixing us with a stare, he said in a loud voice, "We know that not all
of you are really from Western Europe. We cannot take those of
you who are not. I want whoever is really a national of a Western
country to step forward now. You others, stay where you are."

The true Westerners stepped forward. This time, not one of the
rest of us moved. No one wanted to be responsible for upsetting
the transfer. There was a clear risk that if the Swedes couldn't separate us out, they would simply take everyone back to the farm.

Then no one, not even those who were really from the West, would escape.

However, I just couldn't give up so easily. Our lives were at stake. I went up to the man in charge and implored him to take us, too. "Can't you see that without your help, we're condemned?" I gestured to those standing behind me. "Look at the condition of some of these people. If you send us back, they'll be dead tomorrow."

"I don't have enough room on the ship," the man replied. But his objection was absurd. I could see the ship from where I stood. It wouldn't sink with forty more passengers.

"It's only a short trip," I said. "We'll stand on deck. Please take us." I looked at the other two officers. Would they intervene? They didn't say a word. Neither spoke up for us. Instead, they ordered the truck drivers to take us back to Schmidt's farm.

As I climbed back into the truck, I was so discouraged. What had seemed such a beautiful dream—freedom, recovery, a new start, life—had turned out to be no more than just that—a dream. We had had a brief glimpse of freedom, the great white ship in the bay. While I wasn't sorry that some of us were escaping, I couldn't have been more heartsick for myself, Josek, and the rest of us on the truck. I kept my eyes on the ship as long as I could; then we turned a corner and the vision was gone.

Years later, I would learn that someone had betrayed us to the Swedes—but I never learned who. The Red Cross officials, while polite and efficient, had lacked mercy.

Just four days after the Swedish Red Cross declined to rescue us, the SS ferried us out to the *Cap Arcona* and locked us in the storeroom.

Not only on the *Cap Arcona*, but also on the *Athen* and *Thielbek*, conditions continued to be unbelievably miserable for the prisoners.

Athen prisoner Mezmalietis later reported, ". . . on May 1st, which is a holiday for the Germans, we were told that there was no more drinking water. The bodies of those who had died were piling up in the hold, especially since the corpses from the upper hold were also being brought down to us. The cause of death was typhoid fever. By that time I also felt that my strength was at an end. I moved over to the pile of corpses, which at least was not as cold as the metal floor. The only trouble was that quantities of incredibly large body lice moved over from the dead bodies on to those of us who were still alive. They would gather about your waist until you could scoop them up by the handful."

Meanwhile, the British 2nd Tactical Air Force was beginning to assemble in the area. Based in Hustedt, the 2nd TAF consisted of No. 2, No. 83, and No. 84 Groups, and was responsible for the coastal area from Kiel southeast to Poel Island, including Lübeck and Neustadt Bays. The Typhoon squadrons that would appear over Neustadt Bay on May 3 were all in 83 Group. The official RAF narrative of events describes the chaotic conditions in the area at this time: "On the ground the roads were packed with transport of all kinds and with thousands of pedestrians. The scene resembled the Falaise Gap of August 1944, [a break in the Allied lines through which masses of outnumbered German troops retreated] but with an important difference. Among the fugitive troops and civilians were many Allied prisoners of war and displaced persons who had broken out of the labor camps; all were hastening to reach the British lines.

"On 1 May SHAEF sent a signal to the Tactical Air Forces suggesting that they should restrict fighter aircraft from attacks on vehicles and pedestrians. This was in response to an allegation made by the Swedish Red Cross that sixteen motor trucks carrying Allied POWs had been destroyed near Wismar and Schwerin in north Germany during the last week of April." The trucks were Bernadotte's. The "POWs" were concentration camp inmates.

The full text of SHAEF's message reveals profound concern:

> Air attacks by fighter aircraft against Red Cross trucks, POWs and refugees of various nationalities including Swedish, Danish and Norwegian personnel have increased to the point that it endangers the good reputation of the Allied Air Force and has resulted in the cancellation of all distribution by the Red Cross. . . .

According to Red Cross representation in Stockholm 16 of these trucks have been destroyed during week ending April 25th mostly in vicinity of Wismar and Schwarin and a considerable number of Allied personnel have been killed or wounded. [The U.S.] Eighth Air Force has restricted their fighters from attacks against vehicles or personnel on roads. It has been suggested that the Tactical Air Force be similarly restricted except in areas directly in front of our troops. Desire serious consideration of this problem and your remarks and recommendations at earliest possible time.

2nd Tactical Air Force sent the following response:

After discussion with 21 Army Group consider restriction proposed by you would prejudice speedy capture of Lübeck and establishment of Eastern Flank on Wismar-Schwarin line, as it will give freedom of movement to enemy forces which are likely to come into action against our bridgeheads across the Elbe. . . .

Appreciate difficulty regarding POWs and refugees and orders have been issued that fighter [Typhoon and Tempest] attacks by day on movement on roads is to be restricted to MT [Motor Transport] guns and loaded goods trains. At night impossible to distinguish and important that attacks on moving vehicles continue though unobserved pedestrians may also be hit. Probable that only enemy movement takes place at night.

The response clearly indicates the importance of securing Lübeck to the British, despite clear risks to non-combatants and friendly personnel.

The Operations Record Book of 83 Group, based in Süchteln, also describes conditions in the region: "At the beginning of the month [May, 1945] in the area in front of the Group, the enemy armies were being pushed westward by the Russians and northwards by [Montgomery's] 21st Army group, in an area cluttered with German civilians, [d]isplaced [p]ersons of all nationalities, prisoners of war, and military formations using all forms of transport. . . ."

The 83 Group's Summary of Events for May 1 acknowledged that "Traffic was interspersed with [p]risoners of [w]ar moving away from the eastern camps and the location of the Russian spearheads was very much unknown consequently [sic] pilots had to exercise extreme caution in the selection of targets amongst this profusion." This comment acknowledges the challenges facing British pilots while also foreshadowing the disaster of May 3.

Historian John Toland notes that, fortunately for the Allies on the ground,

> . . . only [German General of the Infantry Günther] Blumentritt's depleted army stood between Montgomery and the Baltic. . . . Blumentritt had been waging a gentleman's battle with the British, pulling back with as little bloodshed as possible. Since mid-April an informal liaison had been maintained between the adversaries, and one morning [May 2], one of the liaison officers for the Second British Army came to Blumentritt unofficially and said that since the Russians were closing in on Lübeck, His Majesty's forces wondered if the Germans would allow them to take the Baltic port ahead of the Russians.
>
> Blumentritt, too, preferred to keep Lübeck out of Russian hands and issued immediate orders not to fire on the advancing British.

Montgomery therefore gave his 11th Armored Division, already in Werndorf (some thirty-five miles south), permission to race toward Lübeck.

Montgomery's personal assessment of the military situation on the ground was succinct: "[I]t could now be said that the enemy had decided to abandon the fight, and, apart from small groups of fanatics, nothing more than token resistance was to be expected from the German armed forces. . . ."

On May 2, according to official RAF narrative, "ships of all kinds were pressed into service by the enemy and large convoys began to assemble in the expansive bays of Lübeck and Kiel. It appears that they were preparing to make a dash to Norway from where perhaps they might continue the struggle. Violent storms prevented the No. 84 Group from operating over the Baltic; No. 83 Group had not sufficient resources to make a powerful strike."

That afternoon, Captain Bertram oversaw the pumping of several hundred liters of diesel fuel into the *Cap Arcona*'s tanks. Without serviceable engines, why he should have been ordered to take on so much flammable liquid remains a mystery.

The *Thielbek*, according to prisoner Philip Jackson, who was aboard, finally left Lübeck, "sail[ing] at 1400 hours on the 2nd May 1945. We arrived in Neustadt Bay in the evening of the same day where we saw lying near us the SS *Cap Arcona* and SS *Athen*. We were packed in the holds of the ship without permission to get on deck. We had 200 grams of bread and 1/2 liter of very bad soup per day. The conditions were in fact appalling."

In actuality, the *Thielbek* did not truly "sail." Her steering gear was still inoperable, making it necessary for tugboats to move her.

At about four o'clock that same afternoon, the first elements of the 11th Armored Division rolled into Lübeck, just twelve miles south of Neustadt, over the Herrenbrücke Bridge. They had come at top speed up empty highways, unopposed by German tanks or troops. In the words of Patrick Delaforce, "They accelerated along the smooth spacious autobahn until the average speed of each vehicle had reached 55 mph. A fantastic sight with 200 vehicles, tanks, carriers, or half tracks—all speeding for Lübeck."

On board the *Cap Arcona* and the *Thielbek*, some prisoners were listening to radios belonging to their guards and heard the news. Jubilant, they imagined the British would soon be in Neustadt to liberate them.

British officers set up a temporary headquarters in Lübeck and met with Major Hans Arnoldson of the Swedish Red Cross and P. de Blonay of the International Red Cross, who were already there.

Arthur Dickens, an English journalist posted to Lübeck immediately after the war, recalls being told that, "[It] appear[ed] that several thousand inmates [had been] taken [from Neuengamme] to Travemünde by SS guards, and herded upon three ships, *Deutschland*, *Cap Arkona* [sic], and a smaller vessel. A [Swedish] Red Cross official (most probably Arnoldson) managed to get several of them exempted and on the appearance of our troops in Lübeck, told Faxton and Mackenzie [Canadian journalists] of his suspicions that the SS intended, with the assistance of German submarines lying further out in the Baltic, to dispose of the victims. My colleagues informed a senior [British] officer. He is thought to have got in touch with the Navy, which took steps to intercept the vessels then lying off Travemünde." But did this unidentified officer in fact inform anyone? There is no record of any British ship "intercepting" any of the prison ships.

There is a second report that British officers knew on May 2, a full day in advance of the RAF attack, of the presence of prisoners aboard the ships. Major Noel O. Till, head of the No. 2 War Crimes Investigation Team, charged with investigating the Neustadt Bay disaster after the war, reported that "on 2nd May 1945, when British troops entered Lübeck, the witness [P.] de Blonay [International Red Cross] informed a senior officer present that seven to eight thousand prisoners were on board ships in Neustadt Bay. He describes this officer as [a] brigadier with the name Roberts or Rogers, and mentions the 11th Armored Division. This officer was presumably . . . Maj.-Gen. ["Pip"] Roberts, commanding 11th Armored Division. . . . de Blonay [himself] heard that the message was passed on to higher authority." But was it, in fact? Again, there is no record.

With the British hot on his heels, Dönitz moved his headquarters north from Plön to Murwik, right on the Danish border. The *Patria*, a small passenger ship, became his new command center in the harbor there.

On the evening of May 2, I learned later, while Josek and I were still asleep in Schmidt's barn, never suspecting that we were about to embark on one last march, the Nazis had tried to load even more prisoners on board the *Cap Arcona* and *Thielbek*. These were 1,600 half-starved men, women, and children from the Stutthof concentration camp near Danzig. Polish Jews and Norwegian policemen, they had been traveling across the Baltic in two open barges, the *Wolfgang* and the *Vaterland*, towed by the tugs *Bussard* and *Adler*.

The camp commandant had begun evacuating Stutthof in January. Leaving the sick behind, he had moved groups of fifteen hundred or so at a time out onto the roads. His guards herded the prisoners west. The bitter cold, snow, and constant exposure took tens of thousands of lives. The guards shot those who couldn't keep up, as usual. All in all, some thirty thousand may have died on these marches alone.

By March and April, the Soviets were regularly bombing Stutthof. Hundreds of innocent prisoners died in these attacks. The Soviets had also surrounded and isolated the camp. There were still some four thousand Jewish women and children at Stutthof, too many to evacuate by land. Accordingly, the commandant loaded two thousand of them onto a cargo ship, without passenger accommodations, and sent it west.

Despite the deplorable conditions on board—virtually no food, water, or even sanitation—the captain found no city willing to let him land the prisoners. Allied planes twice attacked the ship, killing crew members and prisoners. Finally, the ship anchored off Kiel. There, in a third air attack, the ship caught fire. As she sank, hundreds were drowned outright in the cargo holds. Others flailed helplessly in the freezing, churning water beside the ship. Just thirty-three of the two thousand are reported to have survived. Horrific in itself, this incident was a foreshadowing of our own fates.

These unlucky prisoners were not even the last to leave Stutthof. The final contingent departed on April 27, when one hundred-twenty police and a contingent of SS guards loaded three thousand unfortunates into three open barges, the *Wolfgang*, the *Vaterland*, and the *Roland*. Tugboats hauled them out of Hela Harbor into the Baltic. The prisoners traveled for five days over the open water. Many died. The guards simply tossed their bodies into the sea. On the way the *Roland* broke loose and went aground on the island of Greifswalder Oie. No attempt was made to recover the barge because it was believed the Russians had already overrun the island.

The *Adler* and *Bussard* towed the remaining two barges, the *Wolfgang* and the *Vaterland*, into Neustadt Bay, arriving late on the evening of May 2. Their crews tied one barge up to the *Cap Arcona*, the other to the *Thielbek*. The guards from the barges then boarded the ships, expecting to offload their prisoners. However, both Bertram and Jacobsen refused to take them.

While what happened next is clear—the barges separated from the ships—there are differing versions of how this happened.

In one report, the guards simply cut loose the barges, eager to get ashore and frustrated that they couldn't transfer the prisoners.

A postwar British report describes another scenario, where the prisoners took the initiative. When their guards boarded the *Thielbek* and *Cap Arcona*, inmates cast off the lines tying them to the ships. They had heard they were not going to be taken aboard and when they saw their guards disembark, they were afraid they were going to be blown up or set afire.

Walter Felgner, Second Officer of the *Thielbek*, describes still another version: "The prisoners began panicking, because the guards had left the [barge]. . . . The prisoners thought they would drown. On Captain Jacobsen's orders, we set the [barge] adrift, and we told the prisoners to stay calm because the wind was blowing them towards the shore. They could use the hatch-planks as oars to speed their journey to land. And they did."

Whatever the actual sequence of events, the barges drifted off, unguided. Some prisoners screamed and cried out in the dark. They didn't know what was going to happen; they didn't know where they were going. Vienna-born Saba Feniger was on one of the barges. She remembers that "the crew abandoned us . . . Norwegian police, prisoners of war [with us], stood on top of the barge and spread blankets between them [as sails]. The wind blew us slowly to shore."

There are some reports that as the barges drifted away, SS guards opened fire from the *Cap Arcona* and *Thielbek*. Some prisoners leapt overboard in terror, into the freezing water, and tried to swim for shore.

At about 0430 hours on May 3, the two barges reached shallow water. Some prisoners got out and pushed the barges toward land. A few swimmers had also managed to make it in. As the boats grounded out and the exhausted swimmers waded ashore, SS troops, marines, and cadets from the U-boat school were waiting for them. The Germans began firing with rifles and machine guns. Hitler Youth and even some townspeople joined in. Fourteen-year-old Hirsch Dorbian, a prisoner, remembered, ". . . the sick and weak were first to disembark. I was one who disembarked early. I remember being put down [by one of the adults] by a tree, where I was able to witness the other people getting off the boat. Then suddenly, out of nowhere, the guards reappeared, yelling and screaming that no one gave orders to disembark. They started shooting at people still on deck, waiting to go down the makeshift gangplank. Hundreds were killed like that."

According to a British report,

> . . .news of [the prisoners'] arrival was soon received by the commander of the Volksturm, Dr. Kaeselau[,] the police station in Neustadt[,] the duty officer in the U-boat school[,] and Kapitaen Leutnant Zieman, the commander of the Sandbergerweg camp. As a result, Zieman sent a search party of marines from his camp to round up the prisoners and return them to the barges. The duty officer at the U-boat school, Korvette Kapitaen Schulze, also detailed Hauptmann Schmidt, the officer in charge of the police contingent, to round up the prisoners and bring them to the U-boat school.
>
> Hauptmann Schmidt [led] his [70 to 80] policemen to the spot where he was told the prisoners were, and with them went some of the SS [40]. In the course of rounding up the prisoners, members of the marines present and the SS fired at and killed a number of the prisoners, both on the shore, in the water, and actually in the barges.

Eva Wollenberger, now of Beverly Hills, remembers, "'. . . finding [ourselves] in shallow water, the male prisoners began to push

[our] barge toward land . . . We were shot at by the Home Guard, the older men and children who were defending their homeland,' Mrs. Wollenberger said. "'But we got to shore.'"

Saba Feniger recalls:

> With the first light of dawn, we could already see that we were close to shore, and we also saw figures in uniform. Even though we thought, Hitler was dead, it's the end of the war, we came where there were Germans again. I managed to get into a rowing boat. I don't know where it came from. I was pulled to shore by others.
>
> Those who couldn't get up quickly enough, those whose legs were swollen [or] who were too weak stayed below deck . . . The Germans came up with machine guns, and machine-gunned everyone who was on the barge. I can hear it, I can still hear it. . . .
>
> And that was not the end. A group of prisoners [was] pushed into the sea next to the barge.... They were pushed into the water and machine-gunned. . . . The water turned red. . . .

Two later reports from on-the-scene observers: "At short range [the Germans] began to shoot people jumping into the sea, then lying on the deck of the barges they emptied their guns into the holds, killing all the remaining persons there."

Then "the police and SS eventually rounded up the prisoners, formed them into a marching column, and [led] them to the U-boat school. On the march from the landing place to the U-boat school, the stragglers from the column were shot by members of the marines."

A young girl, D. Doellefeld, saw an SS man shoot her mother dead before her eyes. Furthermore, "on arrival at the school, though many were in a dying condition and did in fact die, no medical attention was given to them though a large hospital with doctors and nurses adjoin[ed] the very football ground on which the prisoners were kept." This facility was the naval hospital attached to the U-boat school.

Residents of Neustadt have their own memories.

Margot Jany, then fifteen years old, had risen early and walked into town to buy bread. On her way back, she saw "along the whole beach, corpses were lying. . . . An SS man approached me, very proud: 'Don't go along there! I already have shot so many. . . . It doesn't look very good there. Everywhere dead are lying about.' He said that very proudly.

"I only told him, 'I have to go home. I live here.' He answered, 'Then just go.' Corpses were lying everywhere . . . How many, I don't know. I saw so many dead. I don't know if there were a hundred or more."

Fritz Hallerstede, who lived in a house on the shore, reported going out in the early morning: "I myself counted 208 shot and slain prisoners—women, children, men, and old men—that were scattered along the beach and along the road from the shore to the submarine school."

8

A FLYING WRECKING BALL

MAY 3, 1945. MID-MORNING. In the storeroom aboard the *Cap Arcona*, Josek and I were deeply dejected. Our morale had never been lower. Hitler was dead; the war must end soon. Yet suddenly, we had gone from the open air and relative freedom of a rural German farm to the darkness and confinement of a crowded storeroom below waterline in a rusting hulk. How could this be? What could it mean, except the end for us all?

One inmate moaned, "This is it. We won't leave this ship alive." Others nodded in agreement. But I refused to believe them. Weren't we the tough and unyielding? Hadn't we always survived? Hadn't we made it this far?

When the Germans first invaded, I had seen the Nazis hang my best friend, Szymon Trzaskala—along with nine others from my village of Dobra—just to make examples of them. I knew that my mother, Ester, and my sister, Pola, had been taken to the Chelmno camp in Poland, and died either there or en route, from the exhaust piped into the back of the truck in which they were traveling.

I had been imprisoned at, and survived, the concentration camps of Steineck, Gutenbrunn, Auschwitz, Fürstengrube, Buchenwald, and

Dora-Mittelbau. While at Gutenbrunn, I had fallen in love with a beautiful girl named Zosia who lived in a nearby village. At that camp I was still able to find ways to get outside for a few hours to visit her.

At a time when I could barely think of myself as human, she had loved me and made my life worthwhile. We stole some beautiful moments together. Her family even offered me and my father shelter in her basement, but we were suddenly moved out of the camp before we had a chance to take them up on their offer. I had believed I would marry her as soon as I could, but the Nazis took us off in cattle cars to Auschwitz. I never saw her again.

I survived Auschwitz because I was young and had completed a year of dental training. I had a few professional tools with me as a result of my mother's begging me to take them along when I was deported. These included a forceps, a syringe, and an extractor. With these tools and the one year of instruction I had received before the Germans invaded our country, I was able to be helpful. Put to work in the dental clinic, I performed extractions (usually without anesthetic) and assisted with the treatment of gum disease. I treated both inmates and keepers alike. I became known as "the dentist of Auschwitz."

I had watched my father die in a bunk beside my own in the barracks at Fürstengrube after a savage beating from a guard. This was on Rosh Hashanah, 1944. Yet we were still alive, Josek and I. With this simple fact, I fought to keep my faith in the future and in God.

In the bowels of the *Cap Arcona* I lay down on the cold steel floor, finding a place between my brother and another prisoner, whose name I didn't know. Clutched in my hand was a small cardboard packet, containing my entire nest egg—a little over three pounds of twenty-two-karat dental gold, which I had managed to take away from the dental clinic in Auschwitz. In a pocket of my coat was my real treasure—a wedge of bread from the Schmidt farm. I closed my eyes. Somehow, even in that place, I managed to fall asleep.

Although by the beginning of May German ground forces were no longer consistently active, RAF reconnaissance flights from Süchteln described ongoing maritime activity in Neustadt Bay and

Lübeck Bay. The 83 Group reported: "A considerable amount of shipping was seen moving up the Baltic shores from inland lakes and other movement out into the Baltic." In his history of the RAF, Michael Armitage notes, "[I]t was believed [that] German ships were assembling to transfer troops to the garrison in Norway so as to continue the war from that country."

Many made this supposition, but it was incorrect. There was no such operation under way. The ships British intelligence had seen and photographed were transporting German civilians and wounded soldiers from the eastern provinces. They were not carrying high-ranking Nazis or SS troops. While reconnaissance had duly noted the masses of people moving along the roads of Schleswig-Holstein, RAF interpreters did not realize that most were German civilians and Wehrmacht walking wounded, along with some concentration camp prisoners.

Nonetheless, as Typhoon pilot David Ince of No. 193 squadron later explained, "The intelligence information that we had at that time indicated that those ships [that were seen] were going to be used to ferry German forces to Norway to continue the battle. And indeed, that there would be a number of high-ranking Nazi officials and general staff moving north with them." To be sure, Dönitz himself, Himmler, and other high-ranking Nazis were indeed in the area, and moving north—but by land.

The Typhoon Mark 1B—the plane that was to make the attacks on Neustadt Bay—had built itself a solid reputation, but only after a shaky start. Manufactured by the Hawker Company in England, the "Tiffy" was first flown on May 27, 1941. It was 31 feet, 11 inches long, with a 41-foot, 7-inch wingspan. A single 24-cylinder, 2,189-horsepower engine drove it at a maximum speed of 412 miles per hour at 19,000 feet. Although it could reach over 500 in dives, its usual cruising speed was around 200 miles per hour.

Originally armed with twelve Browning 0.303-inch machine guns, it was later converted to four 20-millimeter cannons. By 1945, the Typhoon had been further equipped with racks for two 1,000-pound bombs (up from two 500-pound bombs) or eight rockets with 60-pound warheads. These rockets were important innovations. Air historian Roy C. Nesbit explains, "although much practice was needed before the pilots could master the peculiarities of its flight, the rocket projectile . . . [transformed] the operations of the anti-shipping squadrons and eventually [replaced] the torpedo as the main sinking weapon."

The plane had a clear canopy over the cockpit, which held a single pilot. The nose came in all sorts of strong, bright colors—yellow, orange, glossy black—to help distinguish the plane from German look-alikes, particularly the Focke-Wulfe 190, a coastal raider that it resembled. Early on, British anti-aircraft shot down a few Typhoons before things got straightened out. Several Spitfires also took them out. Nor were Typhoon pilots themselves immune from the confusion. Early in the war, "Fifi" de Saxe of the No. 609 "spotted a Focke-Wulfe 190 flying side by side with [fellow Typhoon pilot] Bob Wilmet one day, and with a warning from de Saxe, Bob broke away and "Fifi" became the first 609 (Typhoon) Squadron pilot ever to fire his guns in anger."

The original Typhoon was, in the words of one aircraft critic, "a technical nightmare." At high altitudes its engine was hard-pressed to maneuver the 7-ton plane, the heaviest fighter-bomber Britain had ever built. The structurally weak tail assembly often simply dropped off, sending planes into death spirals. Ailerons could fall apart in steep turns.

One air historian writes,

> In the first nine months of its service life, far more Typhoons were lost through structural or engine troubles than were lost in combat, and between July and September 1942, it was estimated that at least one Typhoon failed to return from each sortie owing to one or [an]other of its defects. Trouble was experienced in power dives—a structural failure in the tail assembly sometimes resulted in this component parting company with the rest of the airframe. In fact, during the Dieppe operations in August 1942, when the first official mention of the Typhoon was made,

fighters of this type bounced a formation of FW [Focke-Wulfe] 190s south of Le Treport, diving out of the sun and damaging three of the German fighters, but two of the Typhoons did not pull out of their dive[s] owing to structural failures in their tail assemblies.

All in all, twenty-six failures—and fatalities—were recorded.

Although the plane was redesigned to overcome its structural weaknesses, it remained difficult to maneuver because of its weight. Reluctantly, the RAF withdrew the Typhoon from its intended role as an interceptor, reassigning the plane to low-altitude bombing. In the words of writer Alex Rogers, "the aircraft did have some very important strong points, the most important of which was its very high performance at altitudes below 10,000 feet. Combined with some rather awesome fire power, [the Typhoon] was to provide the ideal platform for low-level sweeps against just about anything that came its way. Improvements to the Napier Sabre engine in 1942, along with structural modifications to the tail assembly and fitting of the much improved bubble-type canopy in 1943, was to turn this monster into a flying wrecking ball."

Unacceptable as an interceptor, the Typhoon turned out to be perfect for attacking highly visible targets on land and sea: trains, trucks, oil tanks, docks, and ships.

As one pilot said of the Typhoons, "They were much steadier than a Spitfire or Hurricane. Where a Hurricane was very good, a Typhoon was rock-steady, and when you fired your guns, your aim wouldn't shift at all, whereas the Spitfire gave a lot of vibration which chucked you all over the place. [The Typhoon] could dive and hold its dive without swinging or messing around . . ."

The early-morning hours of May 3 found the freshly-appointed Führer Karl Dönitz en route to his new headquarters at Murwik. After a difficult trip by armored limousine, dodging Allied fire, he arrived at his headquarters aboard the *Patria* at 2:00 A.M. Here the new Führer delegated Grand Admiral Hans-Georg von Friede-burg, appointed commander in chief of the German navy just the day before, to offer the surrender of all German forces to Montgomery at his headquarters on Lüneburg Heath, one hundred miles south. In his directions Dönitz made it clear he was including German forces in the east as well as the west. Despite what he had said to the German people, Dönitz was not, apparently, going to fight to the bitter end.

He was also trying to buy time, as historian Reimer Hansen puts it, "to ensure that as many soldiers and refugees as possible could escape the Red Army. Dönitz wanted to use all the resources still available to him to protect the columns of refugees and support the navy's Baltic transports. In his view, eight to ten days would be needed to secure the Eastern Armies and the fleeing German inhabitants of the Eastern territories behind Anglo-American lines. During this period, military operations were to be continued on the Eastern Front."

At 0400 hours on May 3, aides awakened Typhoon pilots at Ahlhorn, Celle, Hustedt, and Plantlünne. That morning, dawn came slowly. Low, flat, opaque clouds and drizzle screened the sun. Out on the runways, mechanics were already preparing the planes.

Because of reported "large-scale shipping movement away from Schleswig-Holstein ports," according to 83 Group Operation Order No. 71, the objective of May 3rd's "Operation 'Big Shipping Strike' " was to "destroy enemy shipping in the area west of a line projected north and south through Poel Island and northwards to the limit of the radius for safe action." Poel Island lay on the eastern shore of Lübeck Bay, twenty-five miles from Neustadt. Thus Operation Big Shipping Strike involved some three hundred miles of coastline and two huge bays, Kiel Bay and Mecklenburger Bay, encompassing both Lübeck Bay and Neustadt Bay. Separating Kiel Bay and Mecklenburger Bay was the Fehmarn Peninsula, off which lay three hundred-square-mile Fehmarn Island, the northernmost land mass in Germany. Just south of the strait separating the peninsula and the island was the harbor of Grossenbröde. Important military and merchant ships were moored here, with extensive anti-aircraft batteries protecting them. Of all the target areas, Grossenbröde was the most dangerous. In fact, in an attack by twenty-four RAF Tempest fighter-bombers on May 3, eleven would be lost.

Operation Big Shipping Strike would eventually entail over a thousand sorties. An entire chain of airfields ringing the Baltic would launch strikes.

The 2nd Tactical Air Force Summary of Events for May 3 identified targets as "the large concentrations of shipping making their way from Lübeck, Kiel, and Schleswig in the general direction of Norway. The situation was somewhat similar to Cape Bon [from which Rommel's defeated Afrika Corps had tried to escape Tunisia], except that this time the enemy possessed the whole of his remaining fleet of war."

The Summary also noted: "Main interest today centered on the remarkable amount of shipping moving, or preparing to move, in the Baltic waters from Lübeck up the eastern side of Denmark. Many of these ships, which were of all types, from landing craft to 15,000-ton liners, were moving from Lübeck and from Kiel. . . ."

At 0500 hours the briefings began. Intelligence, weather, and operations officers updated targets, landmarks, routes, altitudes, winds, tactics, possible flak, and weather conditions. On the morning of May 3 they explained to those pilots bound for Neustadt Bay and Lübeck Bay that the large number of ships that had gathered in the area was believed to be what was left of the German fleet, military and merchant marine. Onshore they would see Neustadt, a fishing and shipping port. There were docks and U-boats there to attack. However, the primary target was the flotilla of ships. The latest intelligence was that the Nazis were loading up as many ships as they could with SS and important Nazis in order to relocate them to Norway. Since neither the British nor the Americans had any naval vessels close enough to stop them, the RAF would have to do the job.

At Ahlhorn, No. 263 Squadron Leader Martin Rumbold remembered, "[W]e had already received a confidential report that the Nazi leaders wanted to set off to Norway. That was the last country, except Denmark, which they had still under control. From there they wanted to continue the fight."

The briefing officers also cautioned the airmen. The 83 Group Operation Order 72 included the admonition: "Hospital and Red Cross relief ships will be operating in the area. These vessels will be illuminated and are not—repeat, not—to be attacked."

The pilots pulled on their fur-lined boots, donned their flying suits, buckled on their yellow Mae West life jackets, and strapped on their parachutes. They climbed into waiting jeeps, which took them to the runway. The pilots waddled down the line of planes until they came to their own, hauling themselves up onto the left wing, then into the cockpit. They strapped on helmet and goggles, slid shut their canopies, and checked their instruments. Then they taxied out onto the broad concrete runways, joining the long line of planes waiting to take off.

Generally, a full Typhoon squadron consisted of twelve aircraft and eighteen pilots, who flew in rotation. The squadron was further divided into two "flights" of six airplanes each, themselves split into "sections" of three Typhoons. Each section was designated by a different color—red, blue, or green, for instance—so it could be distinguished during radio communications in the air. The squadron leaders were known by the colors of their sections— i.e. "Red Leader," "Blue Leader," etc. On May 3, due to damage and attrition, some squadrons could not launch a full complement of twelve aircraft. One, in fact, could muster just four.

Squadron by squadron, flight by flight, section by section, the Typhoons lifted off.

Once in the air, they headed north, flying the "finger-four" formation adapted from the Germans. Early in the war, Typhoon pilots had flown the traditional single-file "line astern." However, they soon discovered this formation had significant blind spots that enemy fighters could exploit. In the new configuration the squadron leader flew out front, as the longest finger of an imaginary right hand, one plane to the left and lower, two to the right and higher.

The Typhoons' top service altitude was 34,000 feet. On the morning of May 3, because of the cloudy, rainy weather, they flew much lower—at 3,000 feet. Normally, this would have been very dangerous. However, the Luftwaffe was no longer operational and the planes were not flying over known anti-aircraft sites.

RAF narrative confirms that

> Nos. 83 and 84 Groups now operated against the large convoys putting out into the Baltic for Norway. The ships were concentrated in an area about 40 miles north of Kiel to Fehrman Island, situated off the northern tip of Lübeck Bay. Other ships were still waiting to leave Lübeck, Schwerin Bay, and Kiel. In all there were about 500 craft of all descriptions. At SHAEF it was believed that important Nazis who had escaped from Berlin to Flensburg were on board and were fleeing to Norway or neutral countries.
>
> As the Navy was unable to reach the area because of the minefields in the Kattegat [the bay between the Jutland Peninsula and Sweden], an all-out air effort was planned to block this last escape hole. RAF Coastal and Fighter Commands and the Ninth Air Force were called upon to assist 2nd TAF.
>
> No. 83 Group spent the first part of the day around the ports of Lübeck, Kiel, and Schleswig. The two Typhoon Wings of No. 84 Group were moved to a forward airfield on the Elbe so that they could operate over Lübeck Bay. As the ships steamed out to sea they were followed by Typhoons and Tempests. Tempests [actually, Typhoons] of No. 83 Group attacked and hit the liners *Deutschland* (21,046 tons) and the *Cap Arcona* (27,561 tons).

Pilot Peter West of No. 3 Tempest squadron out of Fassberg wrote of the early-morning view from his airplane, on his way to targets near Kiel: "We flew over the coast of Lübeck Bay. It was unbelievable how many ships were anchored there. We saw all kinds of ships—transport, patrol boats. I remember seeing a long line of submarines."

At 1000 hours, Dönitz met with his military and civilian advisers aboard the *Patria*. Although he had already sent von Friedeburg to surrender to Montgomery, if his offer were not accepted, he was ready to consider relocating to Norway. Ultimately he decided to wait for the outcome of von Friedeburg's visit.

Dönitz remained committed to the rescue operation in the east. Peter Padfield writes, "He had no intention of giving up the struggle to save the easterners . . . all naval and merchant shipping that was still serviceable was engaged in a massive 'Dunkirk' operation to bring back soldiers and refugees from the Baltic coast. . . ." Clearly the *Deutschland* was being readied to assist in this effort. A medical team of a surgeon and twenty-five nurses had recently come on board. She was completely operable and she had not taken on any prisoners. Padfield's statement also suggests that the Nazis had no intention of using the *Cap Arcona* or *Thielbek* to actually take prisoners anywhere. Dönitz or Kaufmann would certainly have ordered the *Cap Arcona* east if she could have made the trip. She was, after all, a capacious passenger ship like the *Deutschland*.

At 1130, von Friedeburg, General Hans Kinzel (Chief of Staff of the German Northwest Army Command), and two other officers—among them a Major Friedl—arrived at Montgomery's headquarters on Lüneburg Heath just outside the village of Wendisch Evern. Montgomery had ordered a flagpole erected and a Union Jack run up. When the Germans arrived, he sent one of his assistants to line up the Germans under the flag. They were supremely insulted, as he had intended. When he finally emerged from his tent, he made them stand at attention on the windy bluff while he berated them. The issues were not entirely strategic. "A major!" he fumed. "How dare you bring a major into my headquarters?"

In fact, Eisenhower had already instructed Montgomery to refuse Dönitz's proposition. Accordingly Montgomery told von Friedeburg that he had the authority to accept the surrender of only those forces on his own front. In order to surrender German troops in the east, Dönitz would have to make a full and unconditional surrender, to both the AEF and the Soviets, at the same time. Von Friedeburg saluted and departed. He was back on the *Patria* by late afternoon.

■   ■   ■

There would be four significant attacks on Neustadt Bay on May 3.

The first Typhoons to depart were from Squadron Leader Martin T. S. Rumbold's No. 263 Squadron of eight aircraft, based in Ahlhorn. They lifted off at 1135 hours. With Rumbold were pilots E. A. Tennant, M. S. M. Hamilton, A. R. S. "Ronald" Proctor, J. J. Morgan, L. "Larry" Saunders, L. J. Miller, and D. "Eric" Coles. Their target was the *Deutschland*.

Accompanying them was the No. 609 (West Riding) Squadron from the same airfield: Squadron Leader L. W. F. "Pinkie" Stark and G. F. G. H. A. DeBeuger, A. H. "Lord" Billam, J. DeBruyn, L. B. Bradley, A. G. Laforce, E. L. R. G. Jacquemin, R. D. Harkness, C. H. T. Cables, and A. Gracie.

The ceiling was so low—1,000 to 2,000 feet—and the forward visibility so poor—only out to about 300 yards—that Rumbold couldn't keep his squadron in the finger-four formation. He ordered them into "line astern." When they reached the coast, Rumbold could see the ships below through occasional breaks in the clouds. However, there was not enough visibility to mount an attack and neither he nor his men had enough fuel to wait for the weather to improve. Aborting the mission, they turned back.

In Lübeck, Swedish Red Cross head Hans Arnoldson informed two British officers, otherwise unidentified, that thousands of concentration camp prisoners had been transferred to ships offshore. He is reported to have specifically named the *Cap Arcona* and *Thielbek*. Apparently the officers contacted 83 Group headquarters at Süchteln. It was midday by the time they got through. Officers at Süchteln told them it was too late for their information to be passed on.

Still anchored out in Neustadt Bay, the *Athen* received a radio message ordering her to dock immediately to take on additional prisoners. Captain Nobmann obediently brought her in. However, when he tied up at the pier and saw that he was supposed to board survivors from the Stutthof barges, more dead than alive, he refused. This objection kept the *Athen* ashore, out of danger during the attacks.

No. 184 Squadron, based at Hustedt, ninety-eight miles away, made the second Typhoon sortie over Neustadt Bay—and the first actual assault on the ships. Led by Squadron Leader Derek L. Stevenson, and consisting of just four Typhoons, it took off at 1205 hours. Its target was also the *Deutschland.*

By this time the ceiling had risen to 9,000 feet. Flying over Neustadt Bay at 1,000 feet, the pilots could clearly see the *Deutschland.* The four planes lined up side by side in attack formation, with Stevenson, their leader, on the far right. When the airplanes were almost over the ship, Stevenson radioed, "Going down, going down!" and peeled off the edge of the formation.

As one pilot describes it, "You roll over and down you go [upside down]." Your "port wing flips up . . . and [the plane] accelerates downwards and right . . . Airspeed rapidly increases. [The pilot] keeps the nose well down and peers ahead and through the gunsight glass . . . [He] eases back on the stick, feels the drain of blood from his head, but keeps his eyes fixed on [his target]."

One by one, the Typhoons dived, almost vertically, their speed increasing dramatically from the 250 miles per hour or so at which they had been cruising to over 500 miles per hour.

As the planes gathered speed, the pilots focused on the ship. They didn't look at or think about anything else. As David Byrne of the No. 197 put it, "You're concentrating on your target. You don't want to lose it." Sometimes it was all they could do to stay on course as the planes bucked and bounced from turbulence and sheer speed, their engines shrieking. As the sea rose up to meet them, the pilots stared almost straight down at their target.

Some planes carried gun cameras wired to the 20-millimeter cannons. When the pilots pulled the triggers, the cameras activated, recording the paths of tracer bullets so pilots could later see exactly where their fire had, or had not, landed. Examples give a vivid pilot's-eye view of the scene. The dark hull of the target is clearly visible, but it jerks from side to side as the plane bounces around. The image is blurry, indistinct, haphazard. Smoke from previous hits obscures the target. Clearly, during the few seconds the pilots have to make their attacks, they are under intense pressure.

Compared to large, stationary targets like oil refineries and military complexes, ships were particularly challenging. They were small, thin and mobile. A slight miss on land might set off a secondary explosion which could spread to the target. A miss over water meant a lost bomb or rocket—and no impact on the target. Of course the planes did not have the sophisticated, computer-driven equipment of today. The destinations of their rockets, bombs and bullets were utterly dependent on their pilots' skills. Many missions resulted in huge expenditures of ammunition and the loss of pilots' lives, with little damage inflicted on the enemy.

Stevenson dove until he was just three hundred feet off the water and almost over the stern of the *Deutschland*. Then he fired his rockets. Trailing snakes of white smoke, they shot towards the ship. But Stevenson couldn't wait to see if they hit. He didn't have the altitude. Instead, he pulled his plane into an abrupt, near-vertical climb, back out of harm's way. Momentarily blacking out as g-forces sucked the blood from his brain, he came to a few seconds later, staring straight up at the clouds.

The squadron regrouped. Altogether the four Typhoons of No. 184 had fired thirty-two rockets, their full complement. Three had hit the *Deutschland*.

On board were Captain Carl Steincke, his crew, and the medical team. When the first rockets struck, Steincke and Chief Engineer Adolf Koster were in the captain's cabin debating whether or not they would get any passengers before the British arrived. They were utterly surprised by the attack. However, they reacted quickly and professionally, organizing the crew to extinguish the few small fires caused by the three rockets. Steincke then sent the medical team and crew ashore. He and Koster remained aboard. Earlier, Steincke had ordered the crew to sew white bedsheets together and raise them between the ship's two funnels in a makeshift effort to indicate the *Deutschland* was a hospital ship. The crew had managed to paint a single red cross on the forward funnel before running out of paint

At roughly 1430 hours the nine Typhoons of Johnny Baldwin's No. 198 squadron from Plantlünne, 177 miles southwest, initiated the second attack. Blue Section included Group Captain and

Squadron Leader Baldwin, R. A. Gillam, and P. D. Cross. Green Section was made up of F. B. Lawless, P. W. Millard, and J. E. Scoon. G. S. Chalmers, B. G. Kirk, and W. R. Wardle were the pilots in Black Section.

Their targets were the *Cap Arcona* and *Thielbek*.

9

GOD HELP US!

MAY 3, 1945. EARLY AFTERNOON. Fast asleep on the hard steel floor of the storeroom, my brother Josek beside me, I woke up to a violent *boom!* as a tremendous concussion shook the ship. The storeroom rocked back and forth. Clearly, something on the ship had exploded. I struggled to my feet, the floor tilting beneath me, everyone around me also trying to stand up. Hands grabbed at coats and arms. People lost their balance, or got shoved, and fell back down.

Someone screamed, "They've torpedoed the ship!" What did he mean? The Germans were scuttling the *Cap Arcona?* I'd heard that rumor: we'd been loaded on board not to be taken somewhere, but to be drowned. It seemed too horrific to contemplate.

I headed for the nearest wall, and in order to keep standing, gripped it as best I could with both hands. Josek joined me. The ship was lurching and groaning. Everyone was shouting and screaming. There was a rush for the door, but it was still locked. I could hear people in the corridor outside running by. There seemed to be a huge crowd of them, all shouting.

There was a second explosion, then a third right after it, somewhere above us. Both times, the deafening, low *whump!* was followed by a violent shudder. The room danced around. People fell down. Everyone was screaming—prayers, curses;—the terror was beyond belief. How could it not be? Clearly the ship was being attacked, and we were locked in its belly. No one would come for us. No one would unbar the door. The ship would go down with us inside.

There was a fourth explosion, followed by another violent shudder. This time, the trembling didn't stop and the tilt of the floor increased. Black smoke poured into the room, from where I couldn't see. We all started coughing. The smoke stung our eyes, filling them with tears. Now another panic struck. People cried, "I can't breathe! I can't breathe!" Someone shouted, "We'll all choke to death!"

People were chanting prayers in Hebrew on all sides of me.

I joined a group at the door. As one, we threw our shoulders against it. It wouldn't budge. Some men kicked it, pounding it with their boots. One tried to tear off the handle. Nothing worked. There was no escape. All the time, we could hear people running by outside. We kept calling to them, shouting as loud as we could.

"God help us!" someone cried. "We're going to die!"

The first smoke-trailing missiles that hit the *Cap Arcona* landed between the first and second funnels. The next struck the third funnel and skidded along the Sports Deck. The rockets caused starburst explosions of orange and red flames. Their concussive force rocked the ship from keel to bridge. Shock waves shattered windows. The Sports Deck vaporized. Burning timbers crashed down onto the Boat Deck, and on through to the Promenade Deck, instantly igniting the dry paneling, tables, and chairs inside. The draperies caught fire with a roar.

In minutes the entire upper third of the *Cap Arcona* was in flames. Smoke spiraled up in a huge, twisted column, soon visible for miles. At the waterline, a secondary explosion went off—perhaps a boiler, perhaps the extra fuel which had been pumped on. This burst blew a huge hole in the side, allowing water to pour in.

Johnny Baldwin, the first pilot of the No. 198 to dive on the *Cap Arcona*, was smart and aggressive. He had begun his career by shooting down three German planes in a single sortie. On January

20, 1943, he had engaged them at 20,000 feet as they were attacking London. Shortly thereafter, with two more confirmed kills, he became the first Typhoon ace.

A dashing figure with curly brown hair, a clipped moustache, and a wry grin, he had experienced, according to one historian, "a meteoric rise, going from pilot officer to group captain in just over two years [at age twenty-six]. When his flying training was complete he went straight to an operational squadron, with only 350 hours [of] flying experience."

March 25, 1943 was another memorable day in Baldwin's career. He was shot down over Ramsgate, England, "managing to [bail] out from his burning and spinning aircraft at 1,000 feet. With burnt hands, and unable to deploy his dinghy, he was fortunate to be picked up by an air-sea rescue launch after just thirty-five minutes."

In August Baldwin, along with fellow ace Pat Thornton-Brown, flew the first long-range attack on occupied France—to prove it could be done. In November he transferred from No. 609 to No. 198. Just one month later, he earned his first Distinguished Flying Cross.

Baldwin was also believed to have led the July 17, 1944, attack on Field Marshal Erwin Rommel's staff car outside Vimoutiers, France. Flying one of the two planes involved, Baldwin—or his companion—managed to get a bullet into the driver. As the man collapsed, the car, traveling at high speed, swerved at a right angle across the road, throwing Rommel into a ditch, where he fractured his skull in four places.

While Rommel was recuperating at a nearby hospital, Hitler sent him a personal message. The Führer had discovered Rommel had been part of the group that had tried to assassinate him. Because the Field Marshal was a decorated, popular war hero, Hitler offered him a choice of deaths: he could commit suicide on his own, or be shot along with his immediate family. Rommel had a chauffeur drive him out into the countryside, where he took poison.

Baldwin was confident and flamboyant. He had his monogram, JB, painted on the cowlings of all his planes. He also had it stitched in red and white on his Mae West. He would conclude the war as the overall Typhoon leader, with a record of sixteen individual confirmed hits and one shared. Five of the nine planes in his squadron dove on the *Cap Arcona*, firing all forty of their rockets.

However, No. 198 did not escape unscathed: "[P. W.] Millard's engine cut out and [he] was last seen entering cloud . . . on [his] way back." (Three days later it would be reported that "F/Sgt. Millard returned this evening after his forced landing on the 3rd May; he had made a wheels-up landing on the coast, and by hiding in a mustard field managed to avoid the German SS who were soon looking for him. [H]e waited for the arrival of the British Troops, commandeered a German car, and [drove] back to Base.")

Another British pilot, J. E. Scoon, "forced-landed safely . . . with a Glycol leak." Glycol was an engine coolant.

The remaining four Typhoons from No. 198 attacked the *Thielbek*, firing their full complement of thirty-two rockets. Lacking the superstructure of the *Cap Arcona*, the *Thielbek* didn't catch fire as quickly. However, one of the rockets struck her below waterline. As water poured in she began to sink, listing at a steep angle.

Twenty-eight hundred prisoners were trapped in the cargo holds. Walter Felgner reported that "the *Cap Arcona* was already listing when we were attacked. I saw nothing of the planes, only heard the hits. The bridge was hit. We threw ourselves down. When the attack was over, the sight was horrible. Everywhere human parts, arms and legs, all shot up."

As seawater poured into the holds, the prisoners fought desperately to get out. But the holds were on two levels, and only narrow steel ladders led up. The prisoners climbed all over each other trying to get up the ladders, even pulling down those who had gotten ahead of them. All the time they were shouting and screaming. Those in the upper hold had the best chance, with only one ladder to climb. Those in the lower hold had two ladders. Most of these unfortunates never made it to the upper hold, let alone the open deck.

Prisoner Philip Jackson remembers, "There were hundreds of people struggling to get on deck and there was absolute chaos. Luckily for me I was on deck, and I waited for about five minutes while the ship was sinking to see my father. I did not see him and so jumped overboard."

Walter Felgner recalls a group of prisoners on deck trying to lower two lifeboats. "The after boat was lowered right away, but it was totally destroyed. We then helped to lower the forward boat . . . but we also told them it made no sense. . . . [The boat] was full of holes, shot up, so it would sink at once. The prisoners lowered the boat anyhow, but it sank right away. The prisoners [already] in the water were holding onto any object they could grab. . . ."

Now Rumbold's No. 263 Squadron appeared. After aborting its first sortie, it had refueled at Ahlhorn and taken off again. This was the third attack. "Eight Aircraft took off at 1516 hours to attack shipping in Neustadt Bay," reads the squadron's Operations Records Book. Flying in at 10,000 feet, the pilots dove on the listing *Deutschland*. Anti-aircraft fire, most likely from the *Athen*, just missed them. Altogether, the squadron loosed thirty-six rockets.

They made several hits. One rocket, plunging through the foredeck, exploded below, puncturing the hull at the waterline. The ship rapidly took on more water. Steincke and Koster started the pumps, but they could not keep up. Other rockets struck the superstructure, which burst into flames. Smoke poured into the sky.

Just as on the *Cap Arcona*, the upper section of the ship soon became an inferno of flame and billowing smoke. Steincke and Koster almost certainly perished at this time. Watching through binoculars from the *Cap Arcona*, Captain Bertram saw explosions going off all over the ship.

No. 263's Operations Record Book says simply, "A 10,000-ton motor vessel [the *Deutschland*] was hit amidships and left smoking. Another motor vessel of 12,000 tons [*Cap Arcona*] was seen to be on fire from stem to stern."

Now several prisoners in our storeroom on the *Cap Arcona* tore a wooden plank from an old shelf on the wall. Two of the biggest men picked it up like a battering ram. They ran it against the door as hard as they could. Nothing happened. They tried again and again, but the door wouldn't give.

Meanwhile, we continued to hear explosions overhead. They came regularly. Each time, the ship trembled and the floors and walls shook. Each time, there was an upsurge of shrieks and prayers. Emergency sirens wailed somewhere far away.

Then the room really began to sway, with a slow, deep movement like a giant pendulum. The motion threw us to the floor again. We scrambled back up, only to be sent sliding back and forth across the room, from one wall to another.

The smoke grew thicker. As we fought to keep our balance, we covered our mouths and noses with the sleeves of our jackets. This didn't help much. It was impossible to breathe without coughing or choking. The light went out, plunging us into darkness. The screaming grew even worse.

Suddenly, a bright light flashed where the door was. We could see again. Miraculously, someone outside had unbarred the door and thrown it open. Smoke poured out of our little room. We could breathe! Everyone inside suddenly pushed and shoved each other to get out. I could see—in silhouette—the heads and shoulders of the first group to escape.

In all the confusion, I never saw who opened the door, and I never found out later. Who was there to ask? All I know is, I was—*I am*—extremely grateful. In the midst of terror, deprivation, inhumanity, and outright evil, someone spared a moment for us. Someone gave us a chance. Whatever inspires or drives such people, it is only through their goodness that hope for humanity is preserved.

Josek and I rolled like a ball against other bodies toward the door. In the struggle to get out, I lost track of him. Once outside, though, we met up again. He was waiting for me in the corridor. The passageway wasn't level anymore, but slanted. Black smoke boiled along the ceiling. From right and left people were shoving, elbowing, leaping, and tripping over each other in their eagerness to escape. In the narrow corridor it was all Josek and I could do to stay together. Grabbing each other's sleeves, we clutched them tight so we wouldn't get separated, then fought to make our way through the crowd.

We didn't know the layout of the ship, so we had no idea where to go. People pushed by us, running in all directions. They were just desperately trying to find a way out. Meanwhile, the sirens kept wailing. People shouted back and forth. The floor under our feet continued its slow sideways slide.

"Don't go that way!" someone yelled, suddenly appearing in front of us. "There's no way out! You can't get anywhere!"

We turned around, following him back. After a while we saw a group exploring a side passage. One of them turned, calling excitedly. "There's a stairway here! Come on!"

We ran down this corridor, following the people as they scrambled along, then turned up another passage. Here everyone came to a stop. It was a dead end. The people hadn't known what they were talking about. They ran back the way they had come. We followed more slowly. We didn't know where to go or who to listen to. The smoke in the corridor was getting even thicker and more acrid.

Somehow we found a staircase with brass banisters. Although it was engulfed in flames it was our best chance yet. I told Josek, "I'll try to get to the top. If I can't, I'll come back. If I don't return in two or three minutes, I either succeeded or I'm dead. Then you try."

I took a deep breath, wrapped my arm around my nose and mouth, and charged up the stairs. But I didn't get farther than two or three steps. The smoke was too thick, too harsh. I couldn't see and I couldn't breathe. I stumbled back down, coughing and crying.

What could we do? We couldn't go this way. We couldn't go that way.

Josek and I grabbed each other's sleeves and ran back into the corridor. We tried all sorts of passageways. Then we got lucky. Around a corner we stumbled into the huge, grand dining room we'd come through earlier. There was a lot of smoke, but it wasn't as thick; the ceilings were more than twice as high as those in the corridors. As the ship swayed and shuddered, amazingly, the tablecloths and place settings remained on the tables. However, crystal glasses and pitchers were rolling around on the carpet. I looked around for the stairway we'd come down and saw it across the room. I knew it led to the upper deck, but like the other stairway it was in flames.

Nonetheless, it seemed to be the only way out. Josek and I ran across the room, paused to catch our breaths, and then lunged up the stairs. We got one, two, three, maybe four steps up before the heat and smoke overwhelmed us. Tumbling back down the stairs, we stood gasping in the dining room.

We would have to try something else. But what? Where should we go? *Anywhere but where we've been*, I thought. We ran across the dining room and out a different door from the one we'd come in. Racing down a corridor, we heard some people shouting up ahead. Around a corner, we found a bathroom, its steel door flung open, an excited crowd inside, shouting and shoving. Smoke swirled from the corridor, up, and out through an opening in the bathroom's ceiling. Daylight poured down and in. *Daylight!* Josek and I forced our way in. Someone had lowered two ropes from the upper deck. Everyone in the bathroom was trying to climb them.

I told Josek to bend down in front of me. I clambered up on his back. Others were doing the same. Still others were jumping up, grabbing the ropes any way they could. As I tried to stand, someone pulled me down from behind. I got up on Josek again. Once more someone yanked me back, as another shoved past. It went on like this for a long time; we made no progress at all.

Finally I managed to get hold of one of the ropes. I twisted it around my hand and arm, all the way up to my elbow, so no one could pull me loose. Balancing on Josek's back, shoved this way, elbowed that way, I managed to climb up. Someone on deck grabbed my free hand and hauled me up into the fresh air. I took one gulp, threw the coil of rope off my arm, lay down on the deck, and reached back with both hands for Josek. Someone grabbed my legs, so I wouldn't slip back. There was a boiling sea of hands and faces, a babble of begging voices. Josek plunged forward through the crowd, raising both hands as high as he could. When one of his hands touched mine, I grabbed it with all my strength. Then I got his other hand. I pulled him up, as those holding my legs dragged me backwards. His head came out. Someone grabbed his shirt, hauling him into the daylight.

We got to our feet, trembling and gasping. There was a violent explosion below. The bathroom belched smoke. At the same time, we heard horrible screams. We had got out just in time.

Josek and I dragged ourselves to the edge of the deck. Wrapping our legs around the stanchions, we sat with our feet dangling over the rail, gulping air. I looked out at the harbor. Another ocean liner, which I would later discover was the *Deutschland*, was also in flames. Closer by, I saw a smaller ship, a freighter, listing terribly. This was the *Thielbek*. It was clearly going down. I couldn't believe the number of inmates I saw frantically crawling up and down the ship, or falling off into the water.

Walter Felgner was one of only a handful to survive the attack on the *Thielbek*. He recalled: "At the end Captain Jacobsen, First Officer Andresen, First Engineer Lau, Third Officer Shotmann, and I were standing on the boat-deck. . . . The ship was listing nearly 50 degrees. We were afraid to go into the water, because the prisoners who could not swim were holding on to anything they could grab. Then Captain Jacobsen said to us, 'Go now. The ship is about to capsize.' "

Felgner and Shotmann leapt into the water. As the ship slowly turned over, the cargo on deck broke loose. Huge crates slid from the high side to the low side, crushing prisoners and crew members. Bursting into flames, the *Thielbek* sank to the bottom. With her went Jacobsen, Andresen, Lau, eleven crew, two hundred guards, and twenty-three hundred prisoners.

Only fifty people survived.

She went down at 3:50 P.M. just twenty minutes after the first British rocket hit her.

The 11th Armored was now on the outskirts of Neustadt, just a few miles away, rolling north with the jeeps and soldiers of 6 Commando.

10

HOW COULD WE PART?

MAY 3, 1945. MID-AFTERNOON. Although Josek and I had made it out of the storeroom, we were hardly out of danger. Already at a 30-degree angle, the *Cap Arcona* continued its slow, steady capsize. The entire superstructure was now in flames. Explosions continued, even if we couldn't see them. Clearly, the ship could not stay afloat for long.

What were we to do? We could see the shore, but it looked to be at least a mile and a half away. Could we find a lifeboat? Should we jump in the water? It was freezing. Who could survive for more than a few minutes?

Suddenly there was another explosion, a huge one, from deep inside the ship. The *Cap Arcona* shook as if an earthquake had struck. People screamed. Josek and I gripped the rail for our lives. Some people near us leapt into the water, hoping to escape a fiery death. However, the water was a long way down, and, as cold as it was, could prove just as efficient a killer as fire. Looking over the rail, we saw one after another hit with a splash, then disappear below the surface. They leapt off the deck beside us and jumped out of portholes beneath us.

We watched and watched, but not one resurfaced.

Despite the chaos raging around me on the *Cap Arcona*, I found a moment to look up at the high, wide, beautiful sky. I was so thankful to be out of the storeroom, and out of the bathroom—now an inferno. Josek and I had survived. We were outside, in fresh air, whole and alive. *Why?* I wondered. *Why us?*

I could only imagine a religious answer. The prayers of our loved ones had somehow touched God. He had mercifully intervened. How else could I explain the last hour? Josek and I had been through so much so quickly. Imprisonment in the storeroom. The attack on the ship. Breaking out of our prison. Escaping through flames and smoke. Surviving while others, just yards away, perished in agony.

I sat watching the whole unbelievable scene. As all of these thoughts ran through my head, I still fought to keep my place on the slippery, burning deck, arms around the rail. It was crazy. Smoke, explosions, sirens, flames, shrieks, curses, appeals, booms, shudders, pops (of metal plates), crackles (of walls and furniture). Yet oddly enough, I felt comfortable. Simply put, I was *alive*.

The deck was crowded with hundreds of prisoners. There were also Nazis. I could see a knot of about fifty middle-aged men— Volksturm, probably—at the stern. With them were some women. They looked back and forth between the water and the burning ship, caught in the same fix as the rest of us.

Scanning the bay, I looked for boats coming to rescue us, but I didn't see one. Just a few hundred yards away, the *Deutschland* was also listing and burning. Only one of its smokestacks was still standing, a large red cross clearly visible upon it. Apparently that hadn't been seen by—or made any difference to—the attackers. The other smokestack was a crushed heap of twisted metal. Even at a distance from the burning ship, I could hear the crackling of flames and groaning of metal plates.

Our own ship was clearly going to follow the *Deutschland* and *Thielbek* soon. The deck continued to tilt. Not a lifeboat or life vest was visible. The flames steadily crept aft. More and more prisoners leapt overboard, screaming as they fell. Those who went right down beside the ship had the most trouble. The settling ship had started whirlpools that sucked them up against the hull, then under.

I saw them struggling, kicking, and flailing. I guess they were just too weak from the years of deprivation to resist. They shrieked for help, but there was no one to give it. One after another, they went under. Those who jumped farther out could at least keep their heads above water—for the time being.

Suddenly, I heard a telltale drone overhead. Looking up, I saw a formation of fighter planes appear from the clouds. As they grew closer, I saw the telltale targets of Great Britain on their wings.

"Hooray!" everyone shouted. "They're British! They're British!" Waving madly, we screamed at them. "Hello! Hello! We're prisoners! We're KZ-niks! We're not Germans!" We flapped our black-and-white-striped caps at them. Unbuttoning quickly, we held out our shirts so they could see the stripes.

We had no idea that they had been told we were Nazis trying to escape to Norway. It didn't occur to us that because they were flying at high speed, dodging back and forth to avoid anti-aircraft fire, bouncing around in turbulence, they couldn't see us very well.

To our utter astonishment—and terror—they dove straight at us, one after another. I stood transfixed as they let loose their bombs and fired their rockets. We could follow the path of each one. Some made direct hits on the ship, exploding like thunder, sending whole sections of the upper decks flying into the air. Others missed entirely. Plunging into the bay, they sent up fountains of water that splashed over us and the terrified swimmers nearby. All the while, sirens were wailing, people were shouting and screaming, and the ship was burning.

One pilot flew so low and close I could see his face. I assumed he could also see mine—and those of the other prisoners. *And surely our clothes.* Wasn't it obvious we weren't Germans? Didn't he see we weren't wearing military uniforms? We were prisoners, in stripes. I looked right into the face of our supposed liberator. A young English pilot, my own age. Surely everything was going to be fine now. I had nothing to fear anymore.

Then the belly flaps of his plane opened. The shark-fin bombs fell out one after another. They rained down on the ship. Passing over with an ear-splitting howl, the plane zoomed up and away.

How could he? *Why* would he? The *Cap Arcona* had no armaments. There was nothing for a pilot to fear. Was no one on our side?

Other planes followed quickly. They strafed the decks where we stood, sending us diving for cover. They raked the swimmers beside the ship with machine-gun fire. Screaming with pain and disbelief, they died. The water ran red.

With a sudden lurch, the *Cap Arcona* tipped so harshly Josek and I lost our hold. We slid on our knees down the wet, slippery deck. Scrambling and scratching, we managed to claw our way back up to the railing. We clung to it for our lives. Once again I looked out over the bay. I didn't see a single boat coming out. Of course, we were prisoners—nothings. But there were Nazis on board. And crew. Surely the Germans wouldn't ignore their own people.

Below me, I watched, appalled, as the whirlpools beside the ship increased in ferocity. More and more prisoners were being sucked down. Yet others were still jumping from the decks. Apparently they expected a miracle. They didn't see, as I did, that the few who managed to get away from the ship did not survive. Exhausted by their efforts, they soon went under.

Still another explosion rocked the ship. This time, it was neither a bomb nor a rocket. Somewhere deep inside the *Cap Arcona*, either fuel or explosives had ignited. Orange and violet flames tore up through the ship, and the blackest smoke—like a huge, oily snake—curled up over our heads. The heat was withering.

For a while the deck had been safe, but that was no longer true. The *Cap Arcona* was suddenly more fire than ship. One after another, successive detonations below sent fragments of the ship flying into the air, exploding past our heads.

We couldn't stay. We had to get away.

Josek and I looked at each other. Together, we turned and stared at the shore, a low, dark line of sand, trees and simple houses in the distance. Without saying a word, I knew we were thinking the same thing: I could swim—Josek couldn't.

I might survive in the water. I might even make it to shore. Josek wouldn't last three minutes. He couldn't go over the side.

But how could we part? We'd been together side by side through so much. We were the sole survivors of our family. We were all each other had.

It was one of the worst moments of my life. What else could we do but split up? I couldn't help him by staying. He didn't want me to not try to save myself. I looked down at the gray, hostile sea. Every part of me shivered. It wasn't the cold I thought of. It was the loneliness. *The emptiness.* I would be going alone, without my brother.

I looked up at the sky, as if I might find there an answer to my predicament. Why did I have to make such a horrible choice? Why was I plunging from one horrific situation to another? Why did nothing good ever happen?

Lowering my eyes to the deck, I spied a friend, David Kot, crawling on his hands and knees. He had a length of hawser in one hand, dragging it behind him. Pulling himself up to the rail, he braced himself, then tied one end of the line around a stanchion. He flung the rest overboard. Throwing one leg over the side, he eased himself off the deck, gripping the line with both hands.

I scrambled along the rail toward him.

Looking up, he cried out. "Come down! Come down! The rope will hold you. We have a better chance of being picked up down here!"

I was sure he was right. But what about Josek?

Turning, I called to my brother. "Come on, Josek! We have to go with David! You have to come! If we stay here, we'll be killed by the planes—or the explosions!"

Josek just shrugged his shoulders. He shook his head no. I could tell he was just too frightened. "Berek," he said, using my Polish name, "you go. Maybe you'll find some help out there. I'll wait here."

I still didn't know what to do. I didn't even know what to say. Other prisoners were already going over the side and down David's rope. Clearly they thought it was a good escape route. I couldn't wait much longer. More and more people were noticing the rope and beginning to crawl toward it. I was afraid I might not be able to get on—it would get overloaded.

"Josek, come along!" I called. But he shook his head again. I couldn't persuade him. I took one last look at him, then turned quickly. Our Prague friend Vikky Engel was just going over, and I followed him.

Back on board the *Cap Arcona*, the crew and some of the prisoners tried to put out the raging flames. But when they pulled the fire hoses from their drums, only a few yards came off. Apparently the SS had cut the hoses when they had removed the life preservers and wooden benches. There was no way to extinguish the fires.

Up in the bow, the Russian prisoners were lucky to have disciplined leaders who kept them from trying to escape up the burning wooden stairways. Instead, they led them to steel ladders, by which a large number managed to escape.

Others were not so lucky—even those in cabins or the upper decks. It was not just a matter of going up some stairs. The SS and the Volksturm made every effort to keep back the prisoners. Heinrich Mehringer remembers trying to get from C to A deck. "At the stairs humans were jammed. Shots [were] ringing out. An SS man [was] standing at the top, shooting with two guns into the desperate, pushing prisoners. In his opinion, apparently, the prisoners should remain below—burn or drown. He had hardly emptied his magazines when the angry crowd ran over him."

There were many such harrowing scenes.

One survivor remembers seeing a man stuck while trying to get out of a porthole. The upper half of his body was hanging out of the ship. The lower half, still inside, was aflame.

A group of prisoners desperately tried to lower a lifeboat from davits fifty feet above the water. People were already standing in it. However, those on board couldn't untangle the lines, blocks, and other tackle. The bow of the lifeboat suddenly dropped, while the lines in the stern held fast. Those inside were thrown against each other, screaming. Then flames burned through the stern lines. The boat rolled over, and everyone fell out. As the swimmers thrashed wildly, the bow lines burned through. The boat crashed down on their heads.

Another group managed to lower and climb into three lifeboats. However, the dinghies were hopelessly overcrowded. There were so many people they were stepping on each other's hands and heads. Screaming went on unabated. Suddenly, two of the lifeboats capsized. The survivors swam to the third boat. Fighting to get in, they capsized that one as well.

One swimmer used a corpse wearing a life jacket as a float.

On one deck, a crowd of about two hundred had been trapped by a fireball. They were melted together in a charred clump. Others escaped by running over their heads as if they were pavement.

Faces and arms blistered by fire, some prisoners tried to get up a stairway to the foredeck. Smoke billowed behind them. They shouted and shoved. Suddenly the stairway collapsed, cracking and splintering. Flames engulfed the screaming prisoners. Onlookers lowered a rope, managing to rescue a few.

Second Officer Thure Dommenget remembers Captain Bertram waiting until the very end, then carefully making his way down the anchor chain and dropping into the water. Two small motorboats, used to bring out provisions, were floating nearby. It is believed that Bertram, who survived, got ashore on one of these, the *Störtebecker.*

Dommenget also ended up in the sea. He remembered that "the water was freezing, but my head, sticking out of the water, felt as if it were being fried." He was soon picked up by prisoners who had climbed into the other little boat, the *Kastenbauer,* but could not operate it. His uniform identified him as a merchant marine officer who would know what to do.

11

I WILL NOT LET GO

MAY 3, 1945. AFTERNOON. The rope was wet, cold and hard—rough enough to rip the palms of my hands as I threw my weight on it. I slid down much faster than I expected, landing in a tangle of arms and legs. Entering the water was like sliding into an envelope of ice. The shock took my breath away. I thought I might die then and there.

When I could breathe again, I saw there were six or seven prisoners hanging on. It was all I could do to keep breathing and avoid being drowned by their thrashings. Meanwhile, the suction of the sinking ship twisted us against the hull. Explosions continued to go off. Parts of the ship flying into the air rained down on us.

Saturated with water, my wool jacket was so heavy I could barely move my arms. I wriggled it off. Now I was colder but lighter. I had more strength. Still, I was so cold my arms and legs ached as if they'd been beaten.

"My brother's already come down!" Vikky cried. "He's swimming ashore. Willy's a good swimmer. He'll make it, if anyone can!"

"I hope so!" I replied. We were two friends, clinging to a single rope as we still clung to hope. We were also two brothers who had just been separated from brothers.

Two more came down the hawser. Looking up, I saw other faces crowding the rail. Vikky and I shouted up at them. "No! Stop! The rope can't hold any more!" But the people on deck were desperate—or they couldn't hear us. Another slid down. The rope stretched to the breaking point. I could hear the fibers squeaking.

"Stay off!" we shouted. "*No more!*"

But they kept coming. Soon there were over a dozen in the water, fighting to hold onto the rope. I knew the line couldn't last much longer. I got ready to swim for it. Letting go, I ducked under and grabbed my shoes, pulling them off. I let them fall away into the depths. I pulled off my wool trousers, too. With them, in a pocket, went the dental gold I had brought all the way from Auschwitz—the last thing of value which I owned.

Now I had on only a shirt, sweater, and underwear. I grabbed the hawser, to rest. But the next moment, the overloaded line untwisted like a corkscrew going backwards, then snapped in two.

All of us went under immediately—and together. A jolt of cold went through me. As I fought to get back up to the surface, the water churning and bubbling around me, hands and elbows, knees and feet smashed into me everywhere. I might have been in a giant washing machine. I couldn't see anything but green water and white foam. I lost track of which way was up. I felt I would drown any second. My heart seemed about to burst.

Fighting with everything I had to push away all these arms and legs, I finally thrust my head into daylight. The water broke around me. I had air! Pushing off the people, thrashing wildly with my arms, I gulped it in. I probably took in just as much water. Prisoners were kicking and flailing at each other, out of control. We were all in the same predicament.

We had only our own strength and abilities to keep ourselves up—no lifeboats, life rings, or life jackets. The occasional chunk of wood, drifting by, was quickly grabbed. Otherwise, there was nothing.

Poor David was really struggling. No matter how he beat his arms, he couldn't keep his head above water. He went down, came back up, then went down again. With a final gurgle he went under for the last time. I couldn't believe it. He had found the hawser. He had saved us all. But I didn't have time to think about him for long. All around me, the same thing was happening. Several others who had come down the line survived just minutes before they, too, went under.

The water was so cold I was quickly losing feeling in my arms and legs. My hands and fingers were already numb. Every motion I made sent a block of ice against my chest. I was tiring fast, even though I knew how to tread water. Battling the churning sea was exhausting. The suction kept pulling at me, too.

I had to find something to grab onto. Flinging my arms forward, kicking as hard as I could, I swam right up to the ship, until I was touching the hull. Here, for some reason, the water was calm. There was no undertow. Hand over hand I worked my way along the hull toward the stern. The farther I went, the less turbid and crowded the water became.

When I finally reached the end of the ship, I paused. Holding on to a piece of steel jutting out, I rested. The freezing water had drained me; I felt twice as weak as I would have on dry land. My teeth were knocking together so fast I couldn't control them. My whole body was in convulsions.

All around me hundreds of people were fighting to stay alive in the water. Objects from the ship continued to shower down on their heads. I saw chairs, tables, barrels, crates, window frames—and all sorts of splintered, unrecognizable pieces. Still, no one tried to rescue us.

I looked towards the shore again. Maybe I could have reached it in warm water, but this water was too cold. I knew I couldn't make it. I'd pass out and go under, like all the others. Then I spotted a piece of wood bobbing in the water about thirty yards away. It might have been a log or a piece of the ship. A surge of hope gave me new determination. Shedding the last of my clothes to lighten myself, I set out. Each stroke was a tremendous effort. With every second that passed, the cold stole more of my strength. My muscles stiffened and cramped. Salt water splashed into my mouth, choking me. It was all I could do to get air.

Gradually I closed in on the object, a chunk of mahogany some four feet long—maybe a piece of the railing of the Grand Salon, even. Carving decorated it. Although I was still in the midst of explosions, screams, and crackling flames, I was also in my own little world. All I thought about was getting to this piece of wood. All I cared about was getting my hands on it before I went down for good.

Finally, I reached it. Drawing it under my chest, I lay across it. How my arms ached! Gulping air, I fought to catch my breath. But at least I could rest. At least I was afloat. I would, under no conditions, let go of my piece of wood, I told myself. Aloud I said to the mahogany, "We'll both make it to shore, or both perish. I will not let go of you until you save me."

As I rested I noticed that three long, gray anti-aircraft picket boats had suddenly appeared. Finally, someone was coming to the rescue!

They barreled toward the site of the carnage, slowing only when they came among the shouting, exhausted swimmers.

Their crews hauled aboard SS troops and merchant marine crew, identifiable by their uniforms. Prisoners also made for the boats. Alex Machnew recalls: "The Germans [with rifle butts] hit everyone clinging on [with] their hands, pushing them back pitilessly into the water." When even these blows didn't deter the swimmers, marines on board raised their weapons. "The Germans began to fire. They shot the drifting comrades. Hit by the rapid-fire guns, they sank soundless[ly]."

Some German-speaking prisoners managed to talk their way aboard. Guards later threw them overboard and shot them when they discovered who they were. Philip Jackson had jumped from the deck of the *Thielbek*. He remembers:

> Being a strong swimmer I reached one of the three German launches sent out and was taken on board. Once they knew the people swimming around were prisoners, they merely circled looking for the officers and men of the ship's company and the German guards. They could have picked up hundreds of prisoners but they failed to do this. I even saw them push away prisoners who were trying to get on board.

We eventually got ashore, and about a hundred prisoners were unloaded and were put against a wall of a nearby shed. We thought by the conduct of the German officers and seamen that they were going to shoot us.

There were three further ack-ack [anti-aircraft] launches moored alongside the jetty [where we landed]. These did not attempt to go out to the thousands of people who were swimming around the ships.

The senior naval officer in Neustadt, Kommandeur Fregatten Kapitän Heinrich Schmidt, was commandant of the U-boat school. He later told investigating officials, "[D]uring the attack all available vessels were put into action by me. There were approximately six to eight small vessels. According to statements, checked by me, approximately two hundred humans were rescued."

The truth appears very different. Not only were just three boats sent out, and not only did their occupants repel any prisoners who tried to get aboard, but also many inmates reported seeing the boats purposely run over prisoners in the water. A *Thielbek* survivor confirms that "Three German picket boats came alongside to save the SS and German soldiers who were on the boats. The personnel of these boats fired on the foreign deportees who were trying to save themselves by swimming. There was no attempt at rescue."

Two other Typhoon squadrons followed No. 263, in the fourth, and final, attack on the ships. The first was Squadron Leader K. J. Harding's No. 197, eight Typhoons based in Ahlhorn, but for this mission flying out of Celle, 105 miles away. Besides Harding, the pilots included J. G. B. Hartry, K. K. Walsh, J. K. Byrne, D. G. Lovell, A. R. DeBie, L. S. Brookes, and R. B. Farmiloe. They took off at 1520 hours.

The second squadron was No. 193. Led by D. M. Taylor, this group included D. H. G. Ince, J. Harrison, J. P. Deal, W. Wyse, J. A. Marryshow, M. J. Heald, and R. Chadwick.

Each plane in the squadrons carried two 1,000-pound bombs with high-explosive warheads. The *Deutschland* was the target.

Harding's No. 197 Green Section went in first. Altogether No. 197 dropped eight bombs on the *Deutschland*. Two made direct hits on the already-burning superstructure.

The squadron's after-action report noted: "The attack proved to be quite successful and was directed on a 15/20,000 ton ship. The ship was already burning as the result of a previous attack by No. 263 Rocket Squadron, but two direct hits by No. 197 reduced it to a flaming, capsized hull."

Harding himself reported, "On reaching Lübeck [sic] Bay I saw two very large stationary ships; one [*Cap Arcona*] was burning fiercely, and the other, a large passenger liner with two funnels painted black [*Deutschland*], had a small fire in the bridge. I led Green Section into an attack on this latter from east to west, telling them that 'It would be a shallow dive, as this cloud base was only 2,500 feet.'

"On pulling up from the attack, I saw the first pair of bombs explode on the after hold, blowing a lot of debris out of the port side of the hull. The other bombs all mis-hit. On the next sortie, I saw that the ship had capsized and was still smoking."

By now there were two huge, dark plumes of volcanic-looking smoke boiling up from the burning *Deutschland* and *Cap Arcona*.

Gunners on the *Athen* did manage to take out one of No. 197's planes. The pilot survived: "F/O L. S. Brookes made a forced landing near Neustadt, [apparently on one of the beaches] but happily rejoined the squadron the next day."

No. 193 followed No. 197: "Time up 1515, time down 1635 . . . all the bombs were dropped on a motor vessel of 15/20,000 tons . . . . The ship was already burning as a result of attacks by No. 263 squadron and we scored two direct hits. Now left burning in five places and later seen capsized and burning . . . meager light flak from Neustadt."

Later that afternoon, Harding returned with No. 197, Taylor with No. 193, and King with No. 609, to direct additional attacks on other ships.

In Intelligence Summary No. 266, the Information Officer for 83 Group reported:

■   ■   ■

In what can only be described as brilliant attacks, 9 A/C [aircraft] of No. 198 squadron destroyed a 12,000-ton ship [*Cap Arcona*, tonnage underestimated] and a 15,000-ton cargo ship [*Thielbek*, overestimated]; the No. 197 squadron in Neustadt Bay destroyed a vessel of 15,000 tons [*Deutschland*, underestimated]. . . .

The 12,000-tonner, when left, is reported to have been burning from stem to stern. 2 D/H's [direct hits] with 500-pound bombs are claimed on the 15,000-tonner on which a small fire was burning when No. 197 squadron arrived. As a result of the attack, ship was on fire in seven places and later was soon to be overturned.

From observations of [bailers] out from them, and from the circumstances, it may be assumed that many Huns have found the Baltic very cold today."

In fact, it was thousands of emaciated, exhausted concentration camp prisoners who found the 46-degree Fahrenheit water of the Ostsee cold that day.

Townspeople onshore recall watching in horror as the transport ships burned while people screamed and flailed in the water. But few made an effort to help them.

Among those who did was Franz Wolff, fifteen-year-old cabin boy on the *Cap Arcona*. He had the day off, and was spending it with his family on their tugboat *Aktiv*, which was tied up in Neustadt. When he saw and heard what was happening, he immediately took the boat out to pick up survivors.

Fritz Hallerstede lived in a house right on the shore. In a 1952 statement he said, "[W]e could observe the daily activities on the *Arcona*. . . . Already a few days after it arrived we found out it was occupied by concentration camp inmates . . . Almost daily a barge transported inmates who [were] deceased to be unloaded in the [inner] harbor."

He also witnessed the murder of a group of prisoners from the Stutthof barges. "At midday, about two o'clock [on May 3rd] a group of thirteen inmates [from the barges] was shot in front of my eyes by four navy men and one SS man."

Hallerstede immediately went to the Town Hall to try "to persuade the then mayor and town commandant to do something to stop the massacre. . . .

"Suddenly an announcement came from the submarine school that the *Cap Arcona* was being attacked by enemy planes. We could hear the noise of the rockets and bombs, and rushed to the beach. Here we saw that the *Cap Arcona*, lying near the *Thielbek*, and the large ship *Deutschland* were in flames.

"Horrible screaming filled the air. We saw hundreds jump overboard. Life jackets, wooden planks, and other things were thrown overboard. These smashed those swimmers already in the water, increasing the chaos."

He saw some sort of float with people clinging to it. It appeared about to capsize. He called to his brother-in-law, Hans Frolich, "Come on! We have to go out! They'll drown."

Running down to the beach, the two men launched a little fishing boat. They fought their way through the waves to the float, which they secured with a line. As they towed it in, one of the survivors, wearing a life jacket, went under. The water swirled above his head. "Hold onto him!" cried Hallerstede. One of the prisoners grabbed him and pulled him to the surface.

They passed a stranded U-boat. A Typhoon appeared from nowhere, strafing the submarine. Hallerstede and his brother-in-law remember seeing spurts in the water as the bullets skipped past them.

Hallerstede continues:

> We saw that the *Cap Arcona*, the nearby *Thielbek*, and the *Deutschland* were in flames. On the *Deutschland* were only the crew, who rescued themselves in boats, while on the *Cap Arcona*, where it was said there were six thousand inmates, a horrible panic broke out. We saw that all desperately tried to launch the lifeboats and to reach land in

those. During the attempt most plunged head over heels into the water or remained hung at the bow or stern in the rigging.

Only in the late afternoon did the ship capsize, pulling the majority of the inmates still hanging onto the bow and the stern into the depths. I myself managed to rescue eighteen inmates in a small dinghy from certain death by drowning. . . .

Onshore at the U-boat school, German officers got into waiting cars and fled to Flensburg on the Danish border.

Those prisoners who had somehow managed to survive the bombings, escape the burning ships, avoid the patrol boats, and find the strength to stay afloat, now began to wade ashore on Neustadt's beaches.

They were not met by medical personnel or townsfolk with blankets and food.

Instead, just like the survivors from the Stutthof barges, they were cut down by SS and marines and cadets from the U-boat school. These individuals machine-gunned the inmates in waist-deep water, or waited until they got up onto the beaches to finish them off. One cadre of cadets collected a group of prisoners and marched them back to their compound, summarily shooting those who couldn't keep up or tried to escape. They lined them up, naked and trembling, against a wall.

Dina Huberman, who waded ashore with her sister, "never forgot the moment at the beach at Pelzerhaken when she asked the SS-man 'with the human face' what to do with her sister, too weak to go any farther. Almost every night she dreams about how the man told her to seat her sister below a tree, then took his rifle and shot her."

A marine later remembered: "I saw that people were shot on the beach and thrown into the water. . . . I took my binoculars and could determine that the people shooting were in navy uniform . . . During my observation an officer of our group came, whose name I do not know, and gave us the order to shoot the prisoners that came onshore and were dangerous."

Another cadet corroborated the story. "The members of the rear guard were saying that they shot with machine guns and handguns at running people on shore at the navy school."

After a while, as with the Stutthof prisoners, Hitler Youth and townspeople joined in as well.

12

It Didn't Take Very Long

MAY 3, 1945. LATE AFTERNOON. OFFSHORE. As best I could, I rested on my makeshift mahogany life raft. When I had caught my breath, I started for shore. Clouds of oily smoke continued to pour from the *Cap Arcona*, blackening the air. The flames shot high, crackling. I was so glad I wasn't on the ship. But how much better off was I?

It was hard to make headway. The wood buoyed me up, but it made swimming awkward and difficult. I had to lean forward on it, my head hanging over, and churn my arms on both sides. Of course, I was kicking, too. The waves, two to three feet high, slapped me in the face and pushed me back. I seemed to go up and down more than I went forward.

After a time, I stopped trying to go anywhere. I was just too exhausted. I knew I didn't have the strength to keep this up all the way to shore. The beach was too far away.

While I rested, I wondered what I could do. Not far off, I saw a small motorboat slicing through the waves, an open fishing boat about fifteen feet long. Several people were riding in it. Someone had come out after all! Now, where was the boat headed, I wondered? Fixing on it, I tried to determine its course. Then I plunged forward with all my might, swimming as hard as I could.

I would intercept it! I stretched and kicked, gasped and pushed, surged and stroked. I got a little closer. Now I could see there was a group of eight or nine naked men, people like me. The boat wasn't very big, but it *was* a boat. It was a way I could survive. I redoubled my efforts.

After a few minutes, however, I realized the boat would pass me by. I couldn't reach it in time. I also wasn't the only one struggling towards it. Others were swimming closer to its course. I could hear them crying out, begging to be picked up. I could clearly see the fisherman running the motor, steering the boat. I could make out the faces of the prisoners lucky enough to be on board. I just couldn't get there.

Despair overwhelmed me. This was really the end. I had left the ship. I couldn't get to shore. I wouldn't last in the cold water for long. I was all alone. My last hope, this little boat, would pass me by. But then the boat stopped to pick someone up. Lifting myself as high out of the waves as I could, I waved and shouted. "Help! Help! Save me! *Please!*"

Someone called back. "We can't take anyone! We don't have any room! We're full!"

"No!" I shouted. "Help me! Help me!" I hurled myself forward, thrashing with all my might. At the same time, I kept calling out, frantically.

Finally, I ran out of strength. I just couldn't swim any farther. I couldn't even shout. All I could do was bob in the water, watching the fortunate—those who would live—pass by. Then someone on board yelled, "Wait! It's Berek, the dentist! Let's try to take him!"

My heart leapt. Miraculously, the boat turned toward me. A moment or two later, hands pulled me over the side. I slumped to the floor barely conscious. My arms and legs were too stiff to move any longer. I could easily have passed right out. The floorboards cut into my flesh, but I didn't care. They told me I'd been saved.

The naked comrades and the sunburned man at the wheel were my archangels—truly.

Once the Typhoon squadrons had dropped their bombs and fired their rockets, they might simply have returned to their bases. Instead, at least some of them circled back over the ships. The pilots were pleased with the results of their attacks. As Squadron Leader Rumbold later recorded in his logbook, "We had very good fire going. . . ." They had also suffered no casualties. The only resistance had come from the *Athen.*

Once more the planes plunged toward the ships. However, this time they didn't attack them. Instead, they flew low and flat over the waves, unleashing cannon fire on the swimmers beside the ships. Hitting the water, the bullets kicked up thousands of little fountains of spray.

Prisoner Maurice Choquet, who was in the water at the time, remembers: "I saw people get killed. When they got hit with the bullets, their bodies would jerk and sink into the water."

Survivor Francis Akos, who later became assistant concertmaster of the Chicago Symphony Orchestra, was one of many appalled by the strafing.

Questions may be asked. Was this kind of attack unprecedented? Unusual? Unethical? Illegal? Was it a war crime?

The Charter of the International Military Tribunal of Nuremberg, signed August 8, 1945, defines war crimes as "violations of the laws or customs of war. Such violations shall include, but not be limited to, murder, ill-treatment or deportation to slave labor or for any other purpose of civilian population of or in occupied territory, murder or ill-treatment of prisoners of war or persons on the seas, killing of hostages, plunder of public or private property, wanton destruction of cities, towns or villages, or devastation not justified by military necessity."

The specific issue of the disposition of survivors of wartime shipwrecks had been addressed many times in Europe in the twentieth century. At the 1907 Hague Ten Convention, the United States, Germany, Austria-Hungary, and other countries (but not Great Britain) had signed an agreement on the "rights and duties of the belligerent with regard to individuals." With regard to maritime conflicts, Article 16 stipulated that "after every engagement, the two belligerents, so far as military interests permit, should take steps to look for the shipwrecked and wounded, and to protect them, as well as the dead, from pillage and ill-treatment."

On June 27, 1918, in a famous World War I incident, a German U-boat sank the British hospital ship, *Llandovery Castle*. Hospital ships were protected by international agreement. When the submarine's commander realized his mistake, he ordered his crew to fire on the lifeboats carrying doctors, nurses, and wounded soldiers—so they would not survive to be witnesses against him. Despite his efforts, the occupants of one lifeboat managed to make it ashore. Prodded by the British, the postwar Supreme Court of Germany found that "the killing of defenseless shipwrecked people is an act in the highest degree contrary to ethical principles," and sentenced the commander to a prison term.

In the London Naval Treaty for the Limitation and Reduction of Naval Armaments, of April 22, 1930, eleven signatories, including the United States, Great Britain, and Germany, agreed on certain principles of warfare related to attacks and aftermaths of attacks on merchant vessels and warships. Article 22 stated: "In particular, except in the case of persistent refusal to stop on being duly summoned, or of active resistance to visit or search, a warship, whether surface vessel or submarine, may not sink or render incapable of navigation a merchant vessel without having first placed passengers, crew, and ship's papers in a place of safety.

"For this purpose the ship's [lifeboats] are not regarded as a place of safety unless the safety of the passengers and crew is assured, in the existing sea and weather conditions, by the proximity of land, or the presence of another vessel which is in a position to take them on board."

Did the *Cap Arcona* and *Thielbek* qualify as merchant vessels? The German navy had decommissioned the *Cap Arcona* and returned her to her owners, Hamburg-Süd. The *Thielbek* had never been anything but a cargo ship.

Of course, agreements and protocols of the early twentieth century did not cover the conduct of aircraft, which in those days were too primitive to be in general use.

The London Naval Protocol of 1936 updated the 1930 treaty, but retained the wording of Article 22 verbatim as a special "Procés-Verbal Relating to the Rules of Submarine Warfare."

World War II had its own share of questionable maritime incidents. On September 12, 1942 off West Africa the German submarine U-156 sank the British ocean liner *Laconia*, which had been converted to a transport ship. Eighteen hundred Italian prisoners of war were on board. The U-boat commander called over his radio, in the clear, for help rescuing the survivors.

For the next four days U-156 stood by with three other German ships, pulling survivors out of the water. As they did so, two American airplanes attacked them. Having intercepted the call for help, the U.S. Navy took advantage of the situation.

In response, then-Admiral Dönitz, later Hitler's successor, forbade U-boats to assist survivors of attacks:

September 17, 1942

To All Commanders:

1) All attempts to rescue members of ships sunk, therefore also fishing out swimmers and putting them into lifeboats, righting capsized lifeboats, handing out provisions and water, have to cease. Rescue contradicts the most fundamental demands of war for the annihilation of enemy ships and crews.

2) Orders for bringing back Captains and Chief Engineers (issued previously) remain in force.

3) Only save shipwrecked survivors if [their] statements are of importance for the boat.

4) Be hard. Think of the fact that the enemy in his bombing attacks on German towns has no regard for women and children.

■   ■   ■

For sending this order as well as other actions Dönitz was charged at the postwar Nuremberg Trials, with "waging unrestricted submarine warfare contrary to the Naval Protocol of 1936 . . . to which Germany acceded, and which reaffirmed the rules of submarine warfare laid down in the London Naval Agreement of 1930. . . ." While the Nuremberg Tribunal concluded that despite the "so-called 'Laconia' order of 1942 . . . the evidence does not establish with the certainty required that Dönitz deliberately ordered the killing of shipwrecked survivors. . . . [Nonetheless] the Protocol [of 1936] is explicit. If the commander cannot rescue, then under its terms he cannot sink a merchant vessel. . . . [His] orders, then, prove Dönitz is guilty of a violation of the Protocol."

Of course, while Dönitz's order directly addresses the plight of survivors in the water, it was directed specifically to submarine commanders, not airplane pilots.

On March 13, 1944, U-852, commanded by Capt. Heinz-Wilhelm Eck, sank the British freighter, *Peleus*, transporting wounded soldiers. Eck and his crew knew Allied reconnaissance would eventually spot the wreckage and send bombers to attack them. They also knew they wouldn't be able to evade them unless they obliterated all traces of the engagement. During the night, therefore, U-852 spent five hours machine-gunning survivors in the few lifeboats afloat. They also tried to blow them up. They did not completely succeed.

At Eck's postwar trial, his lawyer, Harold Todsen, argued that Eck's actions were justified because the practices of war had changed with respect to survivors. He cited the British sinking of the German destroyer, *Erich Giese*, on April 13, 1940, off Narvik, Norway. British sailors on the destroyers *Bedouin* and *Warspite* fired on survivors in the water, claiming "operational necessity."

Captain Karl Schmidt of the *Erich Giese* described the incident in a deposition given in Paris on August 23, 1940: "While the crew of some two hundred men was swimming in the water, the British destroyers opened fire against us with machine guns and cannons. Several times from the pressure in the water, I felt the explosion of a shell. . . . Reports made to me by members of the crew after reaching land indicated that a number of soldiers had been hit. . . . Other reports submitted immediately after the battle clearly established that several soldiers were killed while swimming in the water. Those who had been swimming in their vicinity observed that their heads were suddenly all bloody and they ceased moving. According to undisputed testimony, the British also directed heavy fire at the rafts. . . ."

The British maintained that if the German troops had been allowed to survive, they would have rejoined German units in Narvik and reentered the war to threaten them again. Todsen argued that Eck was justified for the same reason; he was just trying to protect his ship and crew. Despite Todsen's efforts, Eck was convicted and executed.

A German defense attorney at Nuremberg quoted U.S. Admiral Chester Nimitz to the effect that "in general [in World War II] U.S. submarines did not rescue enemy survivors if it meant an unusual additional danger for the submarine or if the submarine was prevented from further carrying out its task"—in other words, "operational necessity."

In fact, the practice of attacking survivors was widespread on both sides. According to the U.S. Navy Historical Center, on January 26, 1943 in the South Pacific, the USS *Wahoo*, a submarine under Commander Dudley Morton, ". . . encountered a convoy, sank a freighter and the transport *Buyo Maru*, and damaged another cargo ship. *Wahoo* made additional attacks on a tanker and a freighter." Morton then surfaced to recharge the sub's batteries. At this time his crew began firing on survivors in the water, believing them to be Japanese soldiers. They killed three hundred. Unfortunately, many were Indian prisoners of war. Their justification? To prevent the Japanese from swimming ashore and rejoining their units, only to attack U.S. units once more.

On March 3, 1943 in the Battle of the Bismarck Sea, Australian Beauforts and Beaufighters and U.S. B-17s and B-25s bombed eight crowded Japanese transport ships carrying some seven thousand troops. After they were finished, thirteen other Beaufighters swept in, strafing the ships at deck height.

By March 4, all eight transports had sunk. Allied aircraft returned on this and the next day, strafing Japanese life rafts, lifeboats, and rescue vessels. They were determined to prevent survivors from reaching Lae, a Japanese base eighty miles away, and getting back into the war. Beaufighters and B-25s machine-gunned at least four hundred Japanese sailors and marines. As military historian Brad Manera has said, "It was a horrible task and one that haunted several of the aircrews for years to come."

In short, while protocols for the disposition of survivors of maritime attacks had been set down in various treaties in the early twentieth century, in World War II they were largely ignored by both sides. Furthermore, not only naval vessels but also aircraft were involved in follow-up attacks on survivors. The *Laconia* and Bismarck Sea incidents are significant examples, and they preceded the Neustadt Bay strafing by two years.

Allan Wyse of No. 193 squadron later reflected in an interview for the History Channel film *Typhoons' Last Storm*, "We used cannon fire into the water. Poor chaps. . . . They were bailing out of ships, hoping to be safe in the sea, away from the bombs, and it was our dastardly job to make sure they weren't safe, and we just shot them up with 20-millimeter cannon, and I can't imagine that would have been much fun for those German troops at all. Horrible, really, but that's war. We were told to do it, and we did it. . . . I am not proud of that fact. It still stays with me."

Returning to their bases, the Typhoon pilots were no doubt pleased and relieved. They had managed to destroy 23 ships, among them the *Cap Arcona*, *Deutschland*, and *Thielbek*, while damaging another 115. The final tally would include two tankers, two U-boat tenders, nine destroyers, ten minesweepers, two antiaircraft ships, one dredge, and thirty small craft (trawlers, tugs, fishing boats). They suffered no human casualties.

No. 198's after-action report gives some detail:

Today the weather improved, and 8 [sic] aircraft led by G/Captain J. K. R. Baldwin DSO, DFC went out on a shipping strike in Kiel [sic] Bay. Five aircraft attacked a liner 10,000 to 15,000 tons anchored at OBOE 1140 [coordinate]. This liner received 40 R/P [rocket] hits all over and the vessel was left on fire stem to stern. Four aircraft attacked a cargo vessel 15,000 tons anchored at OBOE 0112. This was left smoking all over listing 30 degrees to starboard, the crew was seen abandoning ship, a further 10,000-ton liner at OBOE 0007, 3 submarines at OBOE 0115, a coaster at OBOE 0917 moving east, tug towing barges east at OBOE 0819 were also seen but not attacked. . . ."

The pilots landed at their air bases sincerely believing they had destroyed the Nazis' last chance to escape to Norway and continue the war.

Squadron Leader "Pinkie" Stark of No. 609 had overflown Neustadt Bay just before noon, noticing the *Cap Arcona*, *Deutschland*, and *Thielbek*. He reported, "I attacked a small motor vessel that had left Lübeck this morning when I noticed three large ships anchored in the bay. They didn't seem to be active, and because the war was ending and there was lack of ship space [for transporting Allied troops], I reported my observation to Intelligence in order to save them. Later on, I was surprised to learn that another squadron had been ordered to attack them."

"It was a terrible thing," Derek Stevenson observed, years later, when he was interviewed for the film *Typhoons' Last Stand* and found out who he had actually killed.

"It didn't take very long," said pilot Peter Deal of No. 193, in a similar interview for the film. The total time of No. 193's sortie was eighty minutes. No squadron was in the air any longer.

As the Typhoons headed home, and the swimmers struggled to stay afloat, the *Deutschland* continued to burn furiously, sending up a thick column of smoke.

At about 4:15 P.M. the *Cap Arcona* finally rolled over. One inmate remembers how a friend and some others had wrapped themselves around the ship's anchor chain to keep themselves away from the flames and out of the water. As the liner capsized, "the chain tightened and squashed the humans against the ship's side."

Quayside, a rocket had finally struck the *Athen*. At that point her crew, the SS, and the Volksturm guards abandoned her. The 1,998 prisoners aboard managed to force open the hatches to the holds in which they were imprisoned. They climbed out, snatched up the food their captors had left behind, and ran ashore. They were on foreign, hostile soil, but they were free.

Mikelis Mezmalietis, a Latvian prisoner on board, remembers:

> All those who could walk or crawl made for the stairs and the only exit from the hold.
>
> I just lay there with my dead companions. About an hour and a half must have gone by. There was a frightening silence. I pulled together my last strength and started crawling toward the exit. Luckily the stairs were made of steel plates, rather than rungs of plain iron bars. I managed to get up on deck. The carefully stretched-out tarpaulins had been cut up and the deck was strewn with punctured bags and scattered rice, sugar, and macaroni. And all this time we had been starving in the holds! I guess my companions had done all this damage before leaving the ship. I was terribly thirsty and looked around for something to drink. Not far away I saw a half-barrel of pickled red beets. I crawled over and drank a good deal of the vinegary marinade. Then I passed out and could have been without consciousness for a while.
>
> I woke up hearing a language I did not understand. [It] turned out to be [coming from] two French students who had come from another [prison ship] looking for loot. Earlier that day they had taken a room in the deserted Marine barracks [at the U-boat school] and were

now scouting around. . . . They carried me to the barracks. . . . I stayed there for two weeks . . .

The 30th Assault Unit was the first Allied ground element to reach
Neustadt and the *Athen*. 30 AU was a special, fast-moving, little-
known naval intelligence unit that traveled ahead of the main
military advance. Deputy Director of Naval Intelligence Commander Ian Fleming, author of the James Bond books, was its supervi-
sor. Historian David Nutting has written, "The 30th AU had plenty
of style. Officially, the unique unit was a tight little strike (bob and
weave) force ordered to get to key, pre-selected intelligence targets
before Allied troops (yes, our own troops) got to them."

In fact, he continues, ". . . by late 1944 ten or twelve splinter
teams were to be found dotted along the line of advance into Germany, each consisting of one or two RN [Royal Navy] (or sometimes USN) [U.S. Navy] officers, with a young Royal Marine
officer and several RM Commandos. Lightly armed with assorted
automatic weapons and traveling in jeeps or armored staff cars,
they dashed from one 'target' to another as the advance progressed
. . . [seizing] anything which could have a naval connection, and
from which valuable information might be gleaned."

A report to SHAEF describes the 30th AU's arrival at the *Athen*:

> A ship called the *Athen* was lying alongside the jetty, and
> was boarded for her charts, which were in fact found to
> contain valuable operational intelligence. . . . We discov-
> ered that the cargo consisted of some 6,000 [actually
> some 2,000] prisoners who were being transported to
> Norway [sic]. They were . . . emaciated and half naked,
> hardly human in appearance. They were of every nation-
> ality: many were Jews, many were political prisoners, and
> one group who struggled to maintain a form of military
> order, when eventually they reached the shore, were sur-
> vivors of *Maquis* [Resistance] prisoners from the occupied
> countries, in particular, from Norway. The German
> guards had fled that [afternoon], giving themselves time

as they went to shoot such of the prisoners as had been stowed on deck, whose bodies were floating in the harbor when we arrived.

I am glad to report that at any rate, two of the SS guards from the *Athen* fell into our hands, and were summarily executed.

Benjamin Jacobs (left) and his brother, Josek. This photo was taken in Germany a year after the tragedy.

Heinrich Himmler, shown here at pistol practice, is often described as the unemotional enforcer of the Nazi policy of repression and extermination.

Female prisoners waited for freedom on the Stutthof barges. They would be massacred in Neustadt Bay on May 2 and 3, 1945.

Prisoners at Neuengamme concentration camp were made to perform hard labor despite malnourishment and illness.

Himmler's order that "No prisoner is to fall into enemy hands alive" provoked many such death marches away from the camps.

A promotional photo of the Cap Arcona.

The Cap Arcona having lost its sheen, was now being used as a transport vessel.

The wreckage of the Cap Arcona after the Royal Air Force attack. There were only 350 survivors.

Only one cemetery in Neustadt, fenced in by stones, has the inscription, JEWISH VICTIMS.

The central monument honoring the dead at the Cap Arcona Memorial Cemetary.

A view of the port today from the Neustadt bureau of tourism.

Vacationers now flock to the peaceful shores of Neustadt Bay, many unaware of the tragedy that occurred here on May 3, 1945.

13

THEY ARE SURELY NO NAZIS

MAY 3, 1945. TWILIGHT. The little boat which had rescued me slowly plowed its way through the waves to shore, its rough diesel engine going *chugga-chugga-chugga*. After a time, I sat up. It was hard to believe my good fortune. I was off the *Cap Arcona*. I was out of the water. I was headed to shore. I was going to live. *I was going to live.*

Of course, we were so loaded down the gunwales were just barely above the surface of the water. We had just an inch or two of freeboard. We couldn't pick up anyone else. Faces in the water begged and shrieked. It was hard to go by them, but the fisherman cautioned us: "We can't take one more, or we'll all go down."

I pulled my knees close to my chest, trying to get warm. Laying my head on them and closing my eyes, I thought of Josek. I had cheated death once more, but he had not. I had a won a victory for myself, but without him, it suddenly seemed hollow.

Our rescuer skillfully ran the boat in to shore, sliding to a gentle stop on a low, broad beach. "Okay, everyone," he said, "you can make it from here."

Gratefully, we climbed out of the boat and waded ashore in the knee-deep water. It was such a relief to feel real ground again. But

I couldn't feel ecstatic, or even happy, only anxious. Turning, I looked back. Dusk was already settling in. The *Cap Arcona* was not easy to make out. But I could see that although it had not sunk, it was still burning. Even though it was over a mile away, the stink of its smoke almost overwhelmed me. Night was coming. *My brother was out there.* I didn't want to imagine what might happen to him. He was the last member of my family.

As for myself, I had no idea what lay ahead. I stood with a group of naked, cold, hungry, emaciated men—all terrified of recapture. We had no idea what to do, what to expect, or where to go.

The fisherman backed offshore, waiting patiently while the last of us waded in. Friendless, without resources of any kind, in hostile territory, we asked if there was anywhere we could find shelter. He thought for a while, scratched his head with his cap, then suggested, "The bakery. Follow the shore until you come to a house on a hill. It's late. There won't be anyone there, but you might find some bread." We thanked him profusely. Waving good-bye, he turned his boat around and headed out to look for more survivors. Like Fritz Hallerstede, he was living proof that not everyone was callous and cruel.

(A handwritten note to Hallerstede and his brother-in-law survived the war. Written by a group of prisoners, the note was inscribed in both English and Russian. Clearly, it was meant for Hallerstede to hand to British or Soviet troops: "The Germans Fritz Hallerstede, Hans Frolich, saved, under danger of their lifes [sic] 17 concentration camp prisoners from the S.S. 'Cap Arcona' and 'Tielbek' [sic] after the sinking of these ships on 3rd May 1945. We would ask, not to do them any difficulties. They are surely no Nazis." All nine survivors signed below.)

We might have done the same for our rescuer. We didn't even learn his name.

I watched him head out. The light had gone out of the sky now. Evening darkened the bay. He would find it hard to locate people. The *Cap Arcona* was almost invisible. From where I stood, I couldn't hear any sound but the hissing of the low surf. After bombs, explosions, machine guns, sirens, and screams, an eerie hush had fallen over the bay. The waves rolled in and out as they had for millennia, even millions of years, as if nothing extraordinary had happened here.

At just about this time, a little after four P.M., the first significant elements of Allied ground troops entered Neustadt—the 11th Armored Division, 159th Infantry Brigade, 15th Scottish Division, 1st Special Services Brigade (including 6 Commando), 1st Mountain Regiment, and 5th Recce Regiment. No. 45 Commando, 23rd Hussars/8th RB, and 2nd Fife and Forfar/Cheshires were also early arrivals.

General Sir John Churcher, Commanding the 159th, described his arrival: "When [we] reached Neustadt, we saw several sunken ships in the bay, and on a spot of land found corpses of displaced persons. They were taken from the ship and slaughtered on land. As it became clear that the Allies would occupy the place, these unlucky people were shot by their SS guards."

Brigadier General Derek Mills-Roberts, commanding the 1st Special Services Brigade, remembered: "When we reached Neustadt we saw several sunken ships in the bay and on one of the headlands many corpses of displaced persons were found: they had been dragged ashore from the ships and butchered. When the place looked [as if it were] being overrun by the Allies, these wretched people had been shot by their SS captors. When 6 Commando, which was in the lead, arrived on top of the hill, this massacre was still taking place, and the Germans, seeing that the tables had been turned, ceased fire and ran toward the new arrivals for protection. A crowd of displaced persons waiting to be butchered immediately turned on their late captors and swallowed them up—it was about the only time in the war that 6 Commando could not raise a gallop to save a situation."

At the U-boat school, the prisoners who had been marched up from the beaches and lined up against a wall got lucky. Just as their captors were about to shoot them, a British tank pulled up. The marines and cadets ran off. A British soldier threw open the hatch and jumped out. He was immediately overwhelmed by grateful prisoners, who grabbed his hands and wrung them.

Bryan Samain, Intelligence Officer of No. 45 Commando, described his experience:

> On May 3 we arrived in Neustadt, a small Baltic port twelve miles north of the great German city of Lübeck, which had been 8 Corps' final objective in the campaign. We did not expect any resistance, and we did not encounter any. Our orders were simply to occupy the town, which we did without any bother at all.
>
> Neustadt, superficially a port whose trade had been crippled by war, proved in reality to be a hothouse of enemy atrocities. A concentration camp was found down at the docks, grossly overcrowded with prisoners of all nationalities, all of whom had been forced to exist on little or no food, and had been subjected to very cruel treatment by their German captors. Several "hell-ships," containing hundreds of political prisoners, most of them dead or dying, were also discovered in the harbor; but the German people, when questioned about these matters, professed complete ignorance.

In fact, Samain had mistaken the U-boat school, to which many survivors had been taken, as a concentration camp. It was an easy mistake to make, since the former cadet barracks were now crowded with emaciated survivors.

Mills-Roberts also reported finding a concentration camp nearby. "By the town was the now notorious Neustadt Concentration Camp, which had almost as unpleasant a record as Belsen—though it could not compare in size. I remember going through the gateway with Jack Christopher and picking up one of the inmates who was as light as a feather: he was dead, but the one next to him was not, and there was very little difference between them." He, too, was actually at the U-boat school.

Colonel John R. C. Christopher of the 1st Mountain Regiment described one of the buildings at the school: "Large numbers lay dead or dying of starvation in a big shed. Several women and children were already dead lying in filthy straw mixed up with those still alive when I arrived. The stench was indescribable. . . . There was no sanitation [;] everywhere there was dirt, filth, and disease."

A survivor later told journalist Arthur Dickens that while the SS and others were shooting those who were trying to get ashore, "troops of the [15th (Scottish) division] engaged in mopping up the area appeared along the shore. A short, fierce battle took place, in which the SS guards were wiped out to a man."

By 1700 hours, 11th Armored tanks were parked in the town square. Major R. T. L. Quail had taken charge of the town. His deputies were Captains A. D. Pratt and E. H. Rockley. In Neustadt, at least, the war was over.

Everywhere along the beaches, as word spread that the British had arrived, the killing stopped. The townspeople and teenagers faded away. The marines and cadets made every effort to blend into the general pool of German troops the British were rounding up. In later years, no one ever came forth to identify individuals involved in the wholesale slaughter of the poor souls who had dragged themselves onto the beaches.

A British officer whose name has not been recorded met in the town hall with Burgermeister Möller. He ordered Möller to call up the commander of the marines at the U-boat school and tell him to bring his troops to the marketplace to surrender—or British troops would attack them. The commander complied. The surrender was effected.

The commanding officer of the 5th Reconnaissance Regiment of the 5th Division, who left a report but not his name in war records, wrote that "on arrival at Neustadt at about 1930 hours I found the following situation. The southern part of the town was held by one Sqn [squadron] of tanks and one Motor Coy [company]. In the town square were some 2,000 [to] 3,000 assorted German army, navy, and air force personnel (prisoners).The town was full of a disorderly crowd of refugees, many hopelessly drunk and all intent on looting.

"Individuals began to come forward with stories of atrocities committed by German marines and SS, but the tellers were all very excited and it was difficult at the time to get a clear picture of what had been happening."

■ ■ ■

Standing on the beach, I raised my eyes to the heavens. "Dear God," I prayed, "my mother and my father and my sister are all dead. Please, God! Let me not mourn my brother, too!"

Then it was time to move on. Everyone else was ready and the air was getting cold. It would soon be completely dark. We were naked and shivering. Together, the ten of us moved off like shadows along the shore, arms wrapped about our chests for warmth. We slid along as stealthily as possible. We didn't want to be seen and captured by any Germans—SS, other Nazis, or locals.

To our shock, we stumbled on the bodies of two comrades from Fürstengrube, lying in the sand. This was a very sad moment. We could not tell how they had died.

Continuing along the shore, we searched for the bakery. Suddenly a figure loomed out of the darkness. A man was walking straight toward us. There wasn't time to run, and nowhere to hide. What would he do? Give the alarm? Call out the SS? Get us imprisoned—or worse, shot?

He was an old man. As we got closer, we saw that he was as frightened as we were. After all, ten strange naked men were striding toward him in the dark. He stopped, eyes wide. Staring, he inquired, "What happened?" When we explained, he was astonished. He hadn't heard anything about the bombing, not even the tremendous noise it had made. We begged him to recruit people to go out and save those who were still alive.

"There's hardly anyone around," he replied. "Most people have left the area because of all the bombing." We parted company and he walked off, shaking his head.

Hobbling along, half-frozen, we met another, smaller group of survivors. Finally, we saw a faint light off the beach to our right. Leaving the shore, we headed straight for it over the low dunes, the saw grass scratching our legs.

After a short hike we made out the silhouette of a little house, the source of the light. Before we reached it, a lingering smell of baked bread confirmed it was a bakery. We tumbled in the door.

Inside a score of other survivors huddled piteously on the floor around two candles. They were wrapped in scraps of burlap and rags, whatever they had been able to find. They were talking about who had drowned and who had made it. Their conversation sounded completely unemotional, as if they were talking about lost objects, not lost people. I listened fearfully for Josek's name to be mentioned among the dead, but it didn't come up. I was determined not to give up hope, no matter how dim his prospects seemed.

On the back wall were three huge ovens, but they were empty and cold. There were faucets with running water, so we were able to slake our thirst. However, we couldn't find any food. Once we got a little warmer, we began to think about our next step. Our biggest worry was being found in the bakery and sent to another camp.

More survivors arrived. The conversation turned to how each one had managed to make it ashore. To a man, each described his experience as "a miracle." Most, it turned out, had been rescued by fishermen. One had seen my friend, Willy Engel, who had set out to swim to shore. "I saw him lying on the beach. He must have made it to the shore, but then he died." He didn't know how. Of course, I was crushed by this news.

All night long, survivors trickled in. Although we were starving, we didn't dare leave to look for food. We were too afraid of being put in another camp.

To my surprise, my friend Mendele even showed up. We called him just by this one name, the diminutive form of his last name. He was younger than I was, a mere fourteen years old, but he had always had "camp smarts" beyond his years. Round-faced, with bright, lively eyes, he knew just how to work—not too hard, but not too little. A smooth talker, he never seemed to get caught when punishment was meted out. Now he had what could have been good news. He said he'd seen my brother still alive on the deck of the *Cap Arcona* when he himself had leapt off the ship.

At 1830, four hours after she had first been hit, the *Deutschland* slowly rolled over and sank to the bottom, a charred wreck.

A light, cold rain began to fall. At around 1900 hours, the British, now in complete control of the area, sent out rescue boats. Lieutenant Commander Blacker of the Royal Navy commandeered two tugs. He also sent out the party boat *Neustadt*, a 45-foot open launch, to the *Cap Arcona*. Although the ocean liner had capsized, she had not sunk. At 84 feet, her beam was greater than the depth of the water, 54 feet, so she lay on her port side on the bottom.

For those who had been able to remain on the ship as it overturned, the British ground forces had not arrived too late. As one prisoner described the scene: "[We saw] the *Neustadt* docking at the foredeck of the giant [*Cap Arcona*]. The docking there was favorable. But eighty-five of us were aft and had to run across the hot wreck forward. The floor was so hot we had to move board before board in order to run across. Everyone helped. Even the weakest were taken."

The British rescued two hundred prisoners from the *Cap Arcona*. After taking them ashore, the soldiers found shelter for them in the barracks of the U-boat school and in the naval hospital. They gave them water and food.

The rocket that had found its way into the hold of the *Athen* either was still smoldering or someone had set the ship afire. In any case, smoke was pouring out of her. Blacker ordered his tugs to tow her out of the harbor, so that no one would be killed or injured if the anti-aircraft ammunition she was carrying exploded. The next day, she went aground on the beach at Pelzerhaken, a mile or so north.

Very late that night the commander of the 5th Reconnaissance Regiment visited the barracks at the U-boat school to see about the prisoners there. His experience was similar to Colonel Christopher's:

> We found one building containing a number of Norwegians. This group was undernourished and living in bad conditions, but were very well off compared with what we found later. We then went to a large wooden hut which was stated to contain Jews. By the light of a torch [flashlight], we saw a mass of humanity crowded together on filthy, straw-covered rags and bits of blankets. The stench

was so foul that it was difficult to avoid being sick. On closer inspection the inmates were seen to be living skeletons with legs and arms little thicker than hockey sticks. On being told that the British had arrived and were going to look after them, they gave a feeble cheer and some of them clapped. It was quite impossible to do anything for them in the dark and they were told to stay where they were until daylight.

As a result of my inspection I sent an urgent message to Division for rations and medical assistance.

14

FREE OF SWASTIKAS

MAY 4, 1945. EARLY MORNING. Dawn broke gray, misty, and wet. To the surprise of all of us in the bakery, two open trucks drove up and stopped in front. A man in civilian clothes hopped out. He strode up to the door, opened it, and without saying who he was or what he was doing, ordered us out of the building and into the trucks. We feared the worst—another camp, or death—so we didn't move.

"Where are you planning to take us?" we demanded.

He looked surprised. "Why, to the hospital, of course. The British are here."

Together, we went outside. Except for a few scraps of wood and clothes on the beach, there was no sign of the previous day's disaster. The sea just rolled in as usual, gulls mewing overhead. We climbed into the back of the trucks, carrying those who couldn't walk because of wounds or exhaustion. Were we really free?

The trucks bounced down a rutted road that ran along the shore. Many dead bodies still lay on the sand. The *Cap Arcona* came into view, lying on her side, a huge, still hulk. I could see no one on her anywhere.

Turning onto a paved road, the trucks sped up. Other trucks rolled by, going the opposite way, painted with large white stars. We chattered excitedly. These must be Soviet trucks, carrying soldiers of the Red Army! Then we saw the soldiers wore dark berets and olive-drab uniforms. They were British. We yelled and waved at them. It was true! The British *were* here! *We were free!* The soldiers must have thought we were crazy—naked men gesturing and screeching from the backs of trucks at them!

Finally, we stopped in front of a large brick building. We were asked to get out. We were indeed at a hospital—in fact, the German Navy's own hospital!

Inside, nurses led us upstairs to a ward, where there were rows of double bunks made up with fresh white linens. Each of us was given a blue nightshirt decorated with the insignia of the German navy—a stylized gold eagle and swastika—and assigned a bed.

Suddenly, we were being given special treatment at an elite hospital. It was a monumental change. I lay on an upper bunk, staring at the ceiling. The nurses dimmed the lights so we could rest. Gradually, I fell asleep.

Sometime around noon two big women in white uniforms brought in a kettle of soup. There were even slices of bread and butter. I ate with relish. Needless to say, I had not had such food in a long, long time. "Just rest in your beds," the women said, smiling, "until the doctor comes. He will be here soon."

The last thing I wanted was to remain in bed. I didn't feel the least bit sick. I was free! I wanted to get out and see the world! But I had no clothes, just the nightshirt. Without clothes, how could I go outside? I called to Mendele, who was on the same ward. After some persuasion, I convinced him to get up and look around for something to wear. I was a grown man, but he was only fourteen. To my way of thinking, as a boy he was more fit to be seen half-naked in a nightshirt than I was.

"Don't worry. I'll scrounge something for you," he said with a grin.

After a long wait, he returned in a black tuxedo complete with tails. It was at least four sizes too big, but he clearly hadn't wanted just ordinary clothes. He had a German naval officer's uniform for me and a pair of boots to go with it.

I was amazed. "Where did you find all this?"

"Don't ask any questions. Just get dressed." He winked.

As we stepped out into the street, he turned and said, almost as an afterthought, "You know what? I saw your brother, Josek."

It was as if he had struck me in the face. I grabbed him by the lapels of his jacket. "You saw Josek?"

"Honest to God. I don't know how he and the others survived. There were about seventy of them. Honestly, I swear by my mother and father, I saw him."

I relaxed my grip. I knew the news had to be true. Mendele wouldn't lie about my brother.

We headed straight for where we thought the center of town was. Along the way, Mendele found a bicycle, which he wheeled along. Two other survivors we ran into also told me they'd seen my brother. By this time, I was very hopeful.

Mendele hopped on his bicycle. We went up a small hill. He rode in circles around me, so as not to get ahead. Up the hill was a group of about a dozen prisoners, still in their striped clothes. In a moment Mendele was among them. As I came forward, he jumped off his bicycle, pulling my brother out of the crowd. I saw Josek coming toward me. Under his arm was a Swiss cheese the size of a wheel.

We embraced. Tears poured down our cheeks. It had been a long time since either of us had cried. Now all the tears, held back for years, came rushing out. We stood in the street in broad daylight weeping like little children.

The CO of 5th Reconnaissance returned to the U-boat school at dawn:

> At first light we started to clear the people out of the wooden hut and another one next to it. In daylight things looked even worse than they had the night before. When all those who could move had been got outside it was found that there were still about 150 inside who were too weak or ill to move and two who were dead. It was obvious that there were many cases of typhus and dysentery. The

worst cases were moved at once to the naval hospital and the remainder waited in the sun until we could get some food for them.

Bakeries in the town were ordered to hand over all their bread and all the milk in the town was commandeered.

Under Lt. Makin, German labor was conscripted to work in the kitchens and by midday a thick soup stew and milk was available for everyone. Many were, however, too weak to come and get it and after having been without food for eight days [probably Stutthof survivors], many were unable to digest the soup, but the thought of food revived everybody's spirits. Further [sic] Germans were conscripted to clean up the town and the barracks area and to start digging latrines, as the sanitary conditions everywhere were appalling.

Later that day, Colonel Christopher visited one of the beaches. "When I arrived on the scene of this outrage with Field Marshal Erhard Milch [the Luftwaffe Armaments Chief, who had been captured in Lübeck] on the 4th May, I saw about 100 bodies, old men, women, and children lying on the beach having been shot in the face at very close range."

Another officer reported,

We found a hastily filled-in grave and a number of corpses lying on the edge of the sea. All these people (and there were women and children amongst them) had been brutally massacred. They had all been shot in the head at close quarters and in many cases had had their heads battered in. Some of them were roped together round the neck and ankles.

In a barge which had drifted ashore were many more in a similar condition, and amongst them we found a girl who was still alive. She had been overlooked earlier in the day as she was huddled up under a blanket against two dead bodies. She was uninjured except for a bad bruise on one hand, but was so weak from starvation that she could hardly talk. She died in hospital some three weeks later.

German prisoners under armed guard were ordered to dig graves and [the prisoners] were given a decent burial.

In fact, all along the shore, on the eighteen miles of beaches east and west of Neustadt, British troops put German soldiers and civilians to work digging mass graves.

Field Marshal Milch had not yet officially surrendered. His capitulation and its aftermath were memorable. F. G. Parson, aide-de-camp to General Sir Evelyn Barker, Commander of 8 Corps, was there. He described the scene in a 1982 letter to London's *Daily Telegraph*:

We had just reached Lübeck . . . when the commander of 1 Commando Bde [then 1st Special Services], Brig. D. Mills-Roberts, sent the general a message that he would like him to come.

The general sent me to meet the brigadier at Travemünde [near Neustadt] on the coast, at the mouth of the river that ran through Lübeck.

The brigadier explained that two Hamburg-American [sic] liners and two large Dutch barges [from Stutthoff] had been used to imprison the unfortunate victims of the concentration camps who had been removed from the path of 8 Corps as it advanced. British intelligence knew of this and warned all concerned but, unfortunately, some RAF Typhoons attacked these ships and set the two large ships alight.

The brigadier took me through Travemünde, a pretty little holiday resort. We walked along the river towards the beach, when we started to find dead bodies, not many at first, but more and more as we came to the beach. When we turned the corner and looked along the beach, we saw that the two large Dutch barges had been blown in and were stranded on the beach, and the two liners were on their sides out in the bay [actually the *Deutschland* had sunk, but the *Cap Arcona* would still have been visible]. The beaches for a good few hundred yards were covered with bodies. I would imagine the figure to be in [the] thousands. The two Dutch barges, which were very deep, had had their ladders removed and it was impossible for the victims to escape. These people had been mown down by machine guns and the brigadier told me that he had found a few survivors in the two barges. Likewise, the bodies on the beaches also bore gunshot wounds.

The children had been clubbed to death and judging by the shape of the wounds, rifle butts had been used. We assume these had been used because the troops concerned were running out of ammunition, but the tragic sight of those small heads bashed in is one I shall never forget.

The brigadier had found out from locals that German marines were responsible for the slaughter. I reported to the general, who came immediately. While waiting for him, Von [sic] Milch, the German field marshal, surrendered to the brigadier [Mills-Roberts], with a *Heil Hitler* and his field marshal's baton in his outstretched hand. The brigadier snatched it out of his hand and broke it over his head. The incident showed how we all felt.

The general ordered me to take the field marshal to see the beaches. I took an interpreter and followed the same route as the brigadier had taken. After [Milch] had seen a few bodies at the river mouth, he asked to be taken back, but I insisted that he should go and see the beaches. When we reached them and all the horror of the incident could be seen, I noticed the field marshal was staggered. He saw how all the people had been killed, and also climbed up onto the decks of the two Dutch cargo barges, and saw for himself the awful carnage that had taken place. He came down from the second barge, and with tears streaming from his eyes, told the interpreter to tell me that he felt ashamed of being a Reich field marshal and a German.

The CO of 5th Reconnaissance reported, "The attitude of the German people was one of complete disinterestedness. The SS were considered responsible—it was nothing to do with the German people and no voluntary offers of help were forthcoming from them. The Western European nationals appeared to have been treated reasonably, but the treatment meted out to Jews, Poles, and other Eastern Europeans seems to have been designed as part of a campaign to ensure their extermination under the most cruel and brutal circumstances."

Just southeast of Hamburg, British forces entered and captured Neuengamme, only to find the camp completely empty and all its records destroyed. Pauly had done his job.

Eventually, Josek described his escape. "About seventy of us were still on the ship, holding onto the railing. It got dark. I thought that was it. But we managed to hang on through the night. At daybreak a boat with English soldiers came alongside and took us off."

The first question one survivor always asked another was, *How did you survive?* No two stories were alike. Unfortunately, there were very few of us now to ask. Most of the tenacious, tough, death-resisting comrades who had miraculously survived years of ghettos and concentration camps, hardened to all that our fierce enemy had handed out to us, had been devoured by the Baltic.

A young British officer with the group asked if some of us would come with him to tell his superiors what had happened. Like most of the other soldiers, he could not believe what we had to say about the camps, or about what had happened offshore. We were the first concentration camp inmates they had encountered.

Josek and I, and two others, all of whom could speak some English, went with the lieutenant in his strange car, a Jeep. Driving west, we passed all sorts of cars, trucks, and even tanks that fleeing German civilians and soldiers had abandoned by the side of the road. We stopped at a small brick post office being used as a temporary headquarters. A middle-aged major with a short haircut and cropped moustache interviewed us. When he asked where we were from, I replied, "France." I had learned it was safest to be from Western Europe.

The major couldn't believe what we told him about the camps and about the bombing of the *Cap Arcona*. He shook his head in disbelief when he heard that British planes had bombed the ships.

When the major had finished questioning us, he suggested we leave the area because of the fighting. Of course, we had no transportation. We asked if we could take one of the many vehicles littering the roads.

"I can't give you official permission," he replied, "but there are so many out there. Just take any vehicle you want. No one will stop you." As for identification papers—"Your tattoos are sufficient," he said.

We were free. Finally. Fully. Just like that!

Along with two others, Josek and I set off down the road, heading west. We checked out every vehicle we came to. Since we knew we couldn't all fit into a car—they were too small—we looked for a truck. We came to a bus, which we tried. However, when it kept stalling, we gave it up. Finally, late in the afternoon, after trying out numerous vehicles, we came upon two little olive-green Fiats with the keys still in them. All day, we had been dulling our hunger with slices from my brother's huge wheel of cheese.

Josek hopped into one of the cars. I took the other.

We drove west, into occupied territory, waving at the soldiers in every British and American vehicle we passed. They must have wondered who on earth were the bony-faced people in striped suits and shabby German uniforms.

Suddenly, we noticed the landscape was free of swastikas.

That same afternoon, von Friedeburg returned to Montgomery's headquarters on Lüneburg Heath. At 1820 hours he surrendered all German troops on the Western front. Dönitz was no longer asking the AEF to also accept the surrender of German troops facing the Soviets, so the offer was now acceptable. Montgomery had had a temporary canvas marquee erected. Inside, BBC microphones rested on a trestle table covered with an army blanket. War correspondents scribbled notes and movie cameras whirred as first von Friedeburg, then Montgomery, signed the instrument of surrender: "The High Command of the Germany Army agrees to the handover of all German forces in Holland, Northern Germany, the Friesian Islands, Heligoland, Schleswig-Holstein, and Denmark. . . ."

The agreement was to go into effect at 0800 hours on May 5.

On May 7 Captain Pratt organized a memorial service for the victims of the Neustadt Bay tragedy. Fifteen British soldiers, rifles at shoulder arms, led a group of survivors and sympathetic townspeople—including women carrying bouquets—from the town square down Heisterbusch Street to a spot on the shore between Neustadt and Pelzerhaken, where three of the mass graves had been dug. They laid flowers on the graves and stood silently on the sand while a Norwegian prisoner led a short service. Survivors were dressed in wool trousers and military jackets of both the British and German armed services—whatever they had been given or been able to find. Captain Pratt also spoke. Then the British soldiers stepped forward and fired a salute over the water.

It was here that the primary memorial to the victims of the disaster would later be built, and here that every year, on May 3, survivors and others return to remember and honor those who were lost.

No one will ever know exactly how many died in the attacks on the ships. The estimate is between seven and eight thousand prisoners. Predominantly Jewish and Eastern European, nonetheless they came from twenty-four different countries: Austria, Belgium, Canada, Croatia, Czechoslovakia, Denmark, Estonia, France, Germany itself, Great Britain, Greece, Hungary, Indochina (the region), Italy, Latvia, Lithuania, Luxembourg, Norway, Poland, Russia, Serbia, Slovenia, Spain, and the Ukraine.

In Rheims, France, on May 7, at 0241, General Alfred Jodl, Admiral von Friedeburg, and Major Wilhelm Oxenius of the Luftwaffe signed the instrument of the unconditional surrender of Germany to the Allies, at the schoolhouse that served as SHAEF headquarters.

The next day, in Berlin, von Friedeburg, Field Marshal Keitel, and General Stumpff of the Luftwaffe, signed the final document of unconditional surrender, endorsed by Lieutenant General Carl Spaatz for the United States, Air Chief Marshal Arthur Tedder for Great Britain, General Jean de Tassigny for France, and Marshal Georgi Zhukov for Russia, to go into effect at 0001 the next morning, May 9.

Over the next few weeks, bodies continued to wash ashore along the eighteen-mile coastline of Neustadt Bay. Naked or in prison stripes, drowned and burned, they came ashore not only at Neustadt, but also at Retti, Pelzerhaken, Timmendorf, Scharbeutz, Haffkrug, Schwamsee, Travemünde, Warm Kemhagen, and even Poel Island, twenty-five miles east. Ninety bodies washed up there. The sands everywhere were covered with rows of skinny, bony bodies with lifeless faces, among them children in shorts. On Timmendorfer Strand the bodies were shoulder to shoulder. The sand could not be seen beneath them.

Eventually over forty mass graves would be dug along the shores of Neustadt Bay.

EPILOGUE:

WHERE THE LIVING MEET THE DEAD

How could such a horrendous disaster have happened? Who, ultimately, was responsible?

On April 9, 1946, at the Hamburg War Crimes Trial, Gauleiter Kaufmann denied responsibility for the deaths of the prisoners. He claimed that the plan was not to scuttle the ships, but to evacuate the prisoners to Sweden. When asked if he knew of an order that stated no concentration camp prisoners were to fall into Allied hands, he replied, "No."

Kaufmann testified that the Gestapo Chief of Hamburg, Gruppenführer-SS Count Bassewitz-Behr, had actually ordered the prisoners onto the ships and was responsible for their deaths.

That same day, in the same court, attorney Kurt Wessig asked Bassewitz-Behr, "What orders did you give?"

Bassewitz-Behr replied that "[I]t was determined during a conference that to leave the camps in the present condition [i.e. populated with prisoners] would not be recommended, and would not be agreeable to the security of the inhabitants of Hamburg. Consequently, the Defense Commissioner [Kaufmann] suggested putting them [the prisoners] on ships."

"Who gave the order for these people to be put on ships?"

Bassewitz-Behr: "I did that."

"Was there an order that the prisoners under no circumstances should fall into the hands of the enemy?"

"Yes."

"Who gave the order?"

"It came from Himmler."

"What does that mean?"

"That no prisoner was allowed to fall into Allied hands."

"If there would have been no possibility for the evacuation of the prisoners, what was supposed to happen to them?"

"According to the order, they should be killed."

Were the Germans really planning to transport the prisoners to Sweden, as Kaufmann asserted? The *Cap Arcona* had already been taken out of service and returned to her owners. If she were truly capable of making a long sea journey, would she not have been still transporting German refugees and soldiers from the east? The *Deutschland* was clearly being readied for just such an effort. She had a doctor and twenty-five nurses on board—but not a single prisoner. The *Thielbek* was not even a passenger ship. It had only emergency steering. If the two ships were going to transport prisoners to Sweden, they would have had to be towed.

Historian Wilhelm Lange writes, "It would have been common practice for the SS to leave the prisoners to drown on board their ships in the Baltic. At this point in the war it already had to be considered a crime to concentrate such large numbers of people on board ships, unless their transportation was of vital importance."

What about scuttling the ships, the scheme that Bertram says he went to Hamburg to protest? In his own words, he asked, "to request release from the order to scuttle the ship in case the enemy approached." While no written document with such an order has been found, Bertram's statement implies awareness of either a verbal or written command. The enemy was definitely going to "approach." It was not a matter of *if*, but *when*.

There was a plan to scuttle ships—U-boats and other German naval vessels—if Admiral Dönitz transmitted the code word *regenbogen* (rainbow). Dönitz never did. However, someone sent the command early on May 5. When the admiral found out, he immediately countermanded the order. Nonetheless, forty ships, primarily U-boats, had already been sunk.

Neustadt was the headquarters of a U-boat school. If the ships were to be scuttled, and their own captains proved reluctant to destroy them, there were plenty of submarines available for the task.

One *Thielbek* prisoner later reported, "Personally, I believe that these boats were intended to be sunk by the Germans. . . . The majority of the SS chiefs were no longer with us. We were guarded by military of the Marine Artillery. We had only [drinking water] for 2 or 3 days brought from camp and the day we were sunk there was no drinking water left."

What about the extra fuel pumped aboard the *Cap Arcona* on May 2? Why fuel a ship that could not sail? Furthermore, why put such a small amount aboard such a large ship? One theory is that the extra fuel was to make the *Cap Arcona* burn faster when she was torpedoed. It is also possible that she was being prepared for one last trip—a very short one—out into deeper water where the beamy ocean liner could actually sink.

A 1947 memo from the Legal Section of the War Crimes Group of the British Army of the Rhine says, "The story of [the Neustadt Bay] case, in a nutshell, was that roughly 7,000 people who had previously been evacuated from various concentration camps had been put on several ships in Neustadt Bay under the most appalling conditions, almost literally packed like sardines, where they were left, obviously in the hope that they would make a target for an Allied attack."

It is impossible to confirm or deny that the Nazis intended to scuttle the ships. On the other hand, if there were really any thought of allowing the prisoners to survive, why were troops sent to machine-gun them as they came ashore?

Today, the official Web site of the *Cap Arcona* Museum in Neustadt asserts that "by positioning the unmarked concentration camp prisoners' fleet with naval military ships, the Nazis created a treacherous trap for the Allies to annihilate the prisoners." The Allies had been bombing ships in the area for days. With complete air superiority and ships still active, why would they not continue to do so? An excerpt from the Operations Record Book of the 2nd Tactical Air Force for May 2 describes a high level of activity in the area: ". . .in the late afternoon two convoys with destroyers and escort vessels were forming up off Neustadt. The amount of shipping was beyond the Group's available resources. Several effective attacks were, however, carried out. Four aircraft of 245 Squadron scored 6 direct hits on a submarine near Travemünde, blowing a six foot hole in the stern. 184 Squadron scored several direct hits on 2 M/Vs [merchant vessels] of 2 and 6,000 tons, leaving them both on fire, and later claimed 2 hits below the water line on a M/V of 3,000 tons. . . ."

On the British side, Maj. Noel O. Till of No. 2 War Crimes Investigation Team "commenced investigations" on June 19, 1945. Among his conclusions: ". . .whatever the ultimate intention, these prisoners were in fact placed on large undefended ships in the middle of a bay, with no adequate life-saving appliances, at a time when all shipping round the coast of Germany was being constantly attacked by the British RAF.

> "It is submitted that this was done either:
> "(a) with the deliberate hope that they would
>   be exterminated by the RAF, or at any rate
> "(b) with such total disregard for their safety that
>   the act becomes an act of manslaughter almost
>   akin to murder."

Till's thirty-page report, issued in September 1945, reflects some discomfort with how he felt he was being asked to conduct his inquiry. He mentions "a much depleted team," explains that "these investigations were interrupted from 6th July to 26th July"; and notes that "on 7th August the Team was ordered once again to drop the case (for another)." Furthermore "on 7th September—a month later—the Investigating Officer [Till himself] with one other officer was allowed a maximum of two weeks in which to complete the investigations as far as possible." Till concludes, "It must be appreciated, therefore, that the investigations have not been as thorough as the importance of the facts warrants. . . ." Nonetheless, the Till Report remains the most complete analysis of the incident.

Till comes across as a careful and thorough researcher. At the start of his report he lists seventy-two transcripts of depositions and reports. He records twenty-two exhibits such as signal messages and photographs. In complaining about insufficient manpower and time, Till could simply be saying what many administrators like to say, or he could be implying to his readers that his investigation had been undercut.

The report's coverage ranges from conditions at Neuengamme to the Neustadt Bay tragedy itself. Till writes, for instance, that "the camp had the usual brothel, but it would appear that there was no difficulty in obtaining women to volunteer to work there as an escape from the alternative hard labor." He also deduced that "between 35,500 to 36,500 male prisoners died during the period of existence of the camp."

On page 13, in item 42, Till reports:

> On 2nd May 1945, when British troops entered Luebeck [sic], witness de Blonay [International Red Cross, Geneva; his name also appears as "de Bronay" and in the List of Witnesses as "P. de Bloncey"] informed a senior officer present that 7,000 to 8,000 prisoners were on board ships in Neustadt Bay. He describes this officer as a brigadier with the name Roberts or Rogers, and mentions the 11th Armored Division. This officer was presumably:—
>
> > Maj.-Gen. Roberts commanding
> >   11th Armored Division
> > Brigadier Churcher 159th Brigade
> > or Brigadier G. Harvey 29th Armored Brigade
>
> who were the three officers entering Luebeck on that day. De Blonay heard himself that the message was passed on to higher authority.

■ ■ ■

Of course the second and third names don't sound anything like "Roberts or Rogers," and neither man had anything to do with the 11th Armored. Furthermore, only Roberts commanded a division. It seems clear that de Blonay passed his information on to Roberts—not anyone else—although Till does not seem to want to say so.

Is Till trying to send us a message here, without actually accusing a superior officer of negligence? Did General "Pip" Roberts fail to pass along the information about the prison ships? De Blonay "heard" the information was passed along, but he does not appear to have been a witness to this transmission—if, in fact, it ever took place.

Here is Till's ultimate conclusion about the responsibility for the Neustadt Bay incident:

> From the facts and from the statement volunteered by the RAF Intelligence Officer [with 83 Group], it appears that primary responsibility for this great loss of life must fall on the British RAF personnel who failed to pass [on] to the pilots concerned the message they received concerning the presence of KZ prisoners on board these ships.
>
> It is understood from de Blonay that certain questions have already been asked by the International Committee at Geneva concerning this aspect of the case.
>
> In view of the grievance which was found to be held by some of the survivors of this disaster at the bombing of these ships by Allied planes, it is strongly urged that an official enquiry be held by the responsible authorities into this failure to pass vital information, as it is understood that no such enquiry has taken place.
>
> It is felt that such an enquiry would go a long way to redress present grievances.
>
> The contents of the above paragraph does [sic] not in any way affect the responsibility of the German authorities for placing these prisoners on board these ships.

■ ■ ■

There is no evidence that the RAF ever held the recommended inquiry.

In Paragraph 52 of his report Till explains how he first discovered the RAF knew the prisoners were on board the ships at least a day before the attack:

> The Intelligence Officer with 83 Group RAF [which sent out the Typhoons] has admitted on two occasions— first to Lt. H. F. Ansell of this Team (when it was confirmed by a wing commander present) and on a second occasion to the Investigating Officer [Till himself] when he was accompanied by Lt. H. F. Ansell—that a message was received on 2nd May 1945 that these ships were loaded with KZ [concentration camp] prisoners but that, although there was ample time to warn the pilots of the planes who attacked these ships on the following day, by some oversight the message was never passed on.
>
> Presumably the message referred to was the one originated by de Bronay [sic].
>
> It should be mentioned that at the time the Intelligence Officer was interviewed, the deposition of de Blonay had not been taken, and until the fact that the message failed to be passed was mentioned by the RAF Intelligence Officer, the possibility of such a thing having happened had never occurred either to Lt. Ansell or to the Investigating Officer.

Till does not name the RAF Intelligence Officer.

A bit later, in finding various Germans at fault, Till names eleven Nazis he deems "responsible for this crime," including Pauly, Kaufmann, and Bassewitz-Behr.

Thus, although Till concludes that RAF personnel on the ground bear "primary responsibility," based on two "volunteered" admissions by "the RAF Intelligence Officer" of 83 Group, he does not name this individual. Is Till protecting him? If so, why? In coming forward, was the officer trying to make sure Till reported the error was with RAF Intelligence, and not, for instance, with General Roberts? I see two possible interpretations—involving either negligence or expediency.

Roberts never passed on de Blonay's information, and the RAF covered for him, through the anonymous Intelligence Officer. In the press of business, perhaps the general simply forgot. Or: Roberts did pass on the information, but the RAF itself was negligent, and through "some oversight," failed to get it to the pilots. But what could this oversight have been? Why didn't the Intelligence Officer define it more specifically? And why did—does—no one seem to want to find out more about it?

The other explanation involves expediency. Roberts passed on the information, but RAF personnel concluded it would not be possible—or too time-consuming—to confirm the report, identify the ships, and restrict them in the time left before the attack. Fearing high-ranking Nazis and SS personnel really might escape to Norway, RAF officials did not want to delay any part of Operation Big Shipping Strike. They decided to go ahead despite the cost to the prisoners. They ordered the anonymous Intelligence Officer to cover for their decision by making sure Till heard that the incident was the result of "oversight," not any conscious decision.

This general approach certainly seems to be reflected in the May 1 exchange of messages between SHAEF and HQ 2nd Tactical Air Force. When queried about restricting its operations because of targeting errors that have "increased to the point that [they endanger] the good reputation of the Allied Air Force," 2nd TAF did reply that the top priority of British 21 Army Group and 2nd TAF was the "speedy capture of Lübeck" and that it was "important that attacks on moving vehicles continue though unobserved pedestrians may also be hit."

In all likelihood we will never know whether or not Roberts passed on the information. If he did, it does not seem likely that the RAF officers would fail to communicate it to the pilots unless they had good reason not to. Concentration camp prisoners were on everyone's minds, as the British and Americans had just recently liberated Bergen-Belsen and Ohrdruf, among other camps. Furthermore, there was ample time to get the message from Headquarters 83 Group to the various squadrons.

While the reader will have to make up his or her own mind, choosing either negligence or expediency, I have to wonder if the second interpretation isn't the most plausible. The RAF sacrificed the prisoners. The presumed relocation of high-ranking Nazis and SS troops to Norway was the priority. From the RAF point of view, the prisoners had to pay the price of preventing the escape. The lead entry for April-May, 1945 in the Operations Record Book of the 2nd Tactical Air Force certainly underscores the RAF's state of mind at this time:

> At about 0830 on [the 3rd of May] recce [reconnaissance] aircraft from 83 Group reported 200+ ships leaving Kiel Fiord, and shortly afterwards other points on the coasts of Schleswig. It was apparent that a large scale evacuation was being attempted, and permission was obtained from ANCXF [Allied Naval Command's Expeditionary Force] to attack. The ships all appeared to be heading in a northerly direction and it was apparent that some were already beyond the striking range of aircraft of the 2nd TAF. . . .
>
> Maximum effort was laid on to these targets, with devastating effects to the enemy shipping.

Denis Richards and Hilary Saunders in their official history, *The Royal Air Force 1939–1945*, support this picture of the RAF mindset: "panic had seized the leaders of Germany, both high and low. Seeking for means of escape, they looked longingly across the Baltic to Norway. Thither they determined to flee and for that purpose, large convoys, amounting in all to about 500 ships, began to assemble in the wide bays of Lübeck and Kiel. For a moment it seemed possible that they contemplated not flight only but the continuation of the struggle. On putting to sea, these convoys were at once attacked by aircraft of the

Second Tactical Air Force. Every effort was made to bring this last despairing move to naught, it being believed that a number of high Nazi officials were in all probability on board several of the ships."

While it is true that Himmler and Dönitz, the new Führer, were in the area, overall the British assessment was erroneous. Eisenhower, of course, had also been convinced that the Nazi leadership and some elite troops were going to regroup elsewhere. Neither the convoys to Norway nor the Redoubt in the Tyrol turned out to be real threats, but it is clear that reasonable individuals *at the time* believed they were.

In fact, the Nazi central command had collapsed. From April through May of 1945, it was every man for himself. Hitler committed suicide, Himmler worked to cut a deal, Dönitz scrambled to keep something—anything—going.

Because the RAF did not follow up on Major Till's recommendation for a full inquiry, because the RAF will not release further records on the incident, and because the RAF has not responded to repeated inquiries over the years, including my own as recently as spring, 2004, I can only conjecture that the prisoners were the victims of a combination of faulty intelligence—about the escape to Norway—and military expediency on the part of the RAF. I wish very much that the RAF would come forward to explain itself after all these years, if not to honor those who died, at least to dispel uninformed criticism. Unfortunately, the RAF does not choose to do so.

Of course Till was not the only one to report that British officers knew the ships held prisoners. Major Hans Arnoldson of the Swedish Red Cross apparently told two British officers. The Canadian journalists Foxton and Mackenzie were reported to have alerted military personnel. It is possible that several sources passed along the information to different contacts in the RAF.

The RAF's official Web site offers a time line of World War II. For May 3, 1945, the entry reads: "Typhoons and Tempests of 2nd TAF [Tactical Air Force] carry out devastating attacks on enemy shipping in the Baltic. Large numbers of flying boats and transport aircraft, attempting a massed [sic] evacuation to Norway, are also destroyed." There is no mention of 7,500 innocent lives lost. The fantasy of the escape to Norway is perpetuated.

On March 20, 1946, in response to a query, Lieutenant Colonel L. E. M. Smith of the War Office wrote to Headquarters, British Army of the Rhine, that "the circumstances of the sinking, which are alleged to be the result of an attack by British aircraft, are being investigated by the Air Ministry and the Admiralty in an effort to obtain any information which may be relevant."

On April 23, P. J. Coles of the Air Ministry wrote back to the War Office: "From all investigations carried out by this section, it is safe to assume that the *Cap Arcona* was in fact sunk by British Typhoon aircraft on May 3, 1945. Several other vessels at that time moored off Neustadt were on the same day, either sunk or damaged. . . ."

Lawrence Bond, writer and director of the History Channel film on the incident, *Typhoons' Last Storm*, reported in a March 2000 interview that the RAF "refuses to release any more information. . . . I asked for more information, but the RAF declined to give it to me on the grounds the investigation was still open—55 years later."

Official British records have three classifications: "closed," "released," and "retained." The first designation means the papers cannot be seen by the public. The second means they have been made public. The third classification means that while certain portions have been made public, other sections, names, or words have not and will not be made available.

Access to records is governed by the Public Records Acts of 1958 and 1967. According to the Public Records Office in London, "the vast majority of records selected for permanent preservation are made available to the public when they are 30 years old . . . . Records may be closed for periods longer than 30 years; this is known as extended closure.

"The release of other types of information may be barred under legislation which overrides the provisions of the Public Records Act. Typical extended closure periods are 50 years, 75 years, and 100 years."

The RAF never told the pilots who they had actually bombed. The airmen only found out years later, by chance. In his 2000 interview, Bond explained that "some of the pilots only learned about what happened when I interviewed them for [my] film."

The men in the airplanes truly believed they were attacking SS troops and high-ranking Nazis who were trying to escape to Norway.

German historian Heinz Schön, author of *Die* Cap Arcona *Katastrophe* (The *Cap Arcona* Catastrophe), places responsibility first on Himmler, then on Pauly, then on the RAF. Because none of the important British books on RAF activities in World War II—books such as Max Hastings's widely known *Bomber Command*—mention the incident, Schön sees a good deal of British guilt about the disaster.

In terms of lives lost, the simultaneous sinkings of the *Cap Arcona* and *Thielbek* represent one of the worst maritime disasters in modern history—if not the worst. Only the sinking of the *Gustloff* compares.

It continues to be appalling that the incident receives no mention in history books. Neither German nor British students learn of the tragedy in school or university.

As the spring of 1945 became summer, Till notes, "from the date of the disaster to 30th July 1945, the total number of bodies washed up on the shore amounted to 253. A further 474 bodies were washed up between 30th July and 10th September, making a total of 727."

He also reports that "in spite of representations having been made by the Investigating Officer to the Military Government Detachment at Neustadt, the burial of these bodies is being carried out in a manner which is regarded as a scandal both by the local populace, the survivors still at Neustadt, and the local British forces.

"They are being buried indiscriminately along the shore on both sides of Neustadt harbor in graves which are not properly marked.

"Bathers are sunbathing on the graves, in some cases in ignorance that graves are in fact there."

As for those who murdered prisoners as they came ashore—from both the Stutthof barges and the prison ships—Günter Möller, the Lübeck public prosecutor charged with looking into the killings, concluded, after decades of investigations, that he could not indict anyone because he had no "clear evidence." "We still don't have the name of a single suspect. . . . It's conceivable that the people of Neustadt thought that they were dealing with criminals. That's maybe the reason why they're not very keen to remember what happened."

The only German imprisoned in regard to the disaster was Captain Bertram, who served eighteen months for accepting an overload of prisoners. When it finally came out that he had been forced to, he was released.

The *Cap Arcona* remained capsized and highly visible in Neustadt Bay until 1950. That year, representatives of the Rolls-Royce Company, which had manufactured the rockets that had sunk her and the *Deutschland*, visited Neustadt to gather data on the effectiveness of their weapons. Their final report showed roughly forty hits on the *Cap Arcona*, causing the "serious fire started in the upperworks which was never brought under control." It also described the particularly effective hit on the *Deutschland*'s foredeck that "passed right through the ship."

After this research was concluded, salvagers broke up the *Cap Arcona* for scrap.

The *Deutschland* remains on the bottom of Neustadt Bay, to this day a popular site for scuba divers. In a 1998 article in *Diver* magazine, Briton Max MacLeod described diving on the *Deutschland*: "We saw a jackboot, shoes, block and tackle, and a crushed tin box. Later, as our eyes became more accustomed to the gloom, we were able to make out a thigh bone here, a pelvis there. . . . This is the real mud and guts of an ugly history hidden from all except divers. I have dived wrecks where there has been a massive loss of life before without feeling the horror I felt in Neustadt Bay."

On February 8, 1950, cranes raised the *Thielbek* from the depths of the bay. Tugs towed her into Neustadt to be repaired and recommissioned. Bodies were still aboard.

The German newspaper *Die Welt* reported: "Walls, decks, and lines are covered with mussels and algae. On deck is chaos. As if destroyed by a giant fist, the remains of anti-aircraft [guns] are hanging overboard. In the interior of the ship horror reigns. In the corners of two [holds] ghostly, bleached bones glimmer and disappear, as if in twilight. . . .

"Shocked, with tears in their eyes, the first visitors are standing there at the place of horror. Hundreds are surrounding on Tuesday afternoon the shores of the Trave during the arrival of the wreck. Hundreds are honoring the victims with a minute of silence."

The remains of forty-nine bodies discovered on board were buried in the *Cap Arcona* cemetery ashore. The ship was subsequently sold twice, sailing under Panamanian registry as first *Magdalene*, then *Old Warrior*. In 1974 she was scrapped in Split, Yugoslavia.

The USSR took the *Athen* as a war prize, renaming her *General Brusilow*. She saw service for Poland as the *Warynski* before ending her days as a floating warehouse in Stettin.

On May 21 Allied soldiers arrested Himmler disguised in the uniform of a police sergeant, as he was attempting to flee south from Flensburg. However, his captors did not recognize him. Two days later he identified himself at the camp near Bremen to which he had been sent. No one knows why. It is likely he believed he would be an important resource for the Allies in governing postwar Germany.

Before his official interrogation, a British physician stripsearched him. The Allies had already lost one high-ranking Nazi to a cyanide capsule suicide. The doctor found a small black knob in Himmler's mouth. It was the stopper to a glass phial of potassium cyanide. As the doctor reached in to remove it, Himmler "jerked his head away to the side, flicked the phial out with his tongue, and crushed it between his teeth." The British made frantic efforts to keep him alive, but he died within minutes.

A Sergeant-Major Austin buried him on Lüneburg Heath in a location he never disclosed.

In the Hamburg War Crimes trial of March through June, 1946, Max Pauly was found guilty of placing the prisoners on the ships— among many other charges—and was hung in Hameln Prison on August 8, 1946, along with eleven of his officers.

Commandant of Neustadt Heinrich Schmidt was tried on charges of shooting prisoners, among other accusations, and was acquitted.

As for Max Schmidt, the commandant of my own group of prisoners, I ran into him again on the very night Josek and I left Neustadt. For some reason, as the sun was setting, we decided to revisit the farm where he had held us. There we were astonished to find some prisoners who had survived by hiding in the area. Even more astonishing, Schmidt's elderly parents invited us to dinner. They slaughtered and roasted a pig. They laid out their best stemware and china. In the middle of this banquet Schmidt himself walked in. He had shaved his head. He showed us a fake KZ number he had inked on his arm. He explained he would try to persuade the Allies that he was a victim, not a perpetrator. Appalled and revolted, we left immediately.

Schmidt laid low after the war, moving to Ibben Beuren. The coal mining there may have attracted him. He took the name "Max Hinz." In 1950, when his father became ill, he returned home, paying a small fine to resume his former identity.

In 1964 a preliminary investigation was opened into his wartime activities. Testimony included the following charges: Schmidt had shot exhausted inmates, killed a prisoner returning from work, shot a Jewish attorney from Czechoslovakia, shot twenty inmates pulling a wagon loaded with rations because they were exhausted, executed inmates unable to keep up on the death marches, ordered the shooting of inmates he had found hiding in a barn, and borne silent witness to many shootings on death marches, including the ones Josek and I had made with him.

Despite the willingness of fifty-two witnesses to testify to various murders or atrocities, Schmidt never stood trial. I made written testimony to the effect that I had seen Schmidt kill a wounded inmate in the infirmary at Furstengrübe, but my testimony never surfaced at the hearing on his case held in Kiel in 1979.

Dismissing Schmidt's case on April 19 of that year the Minister of Justice wrote, "the witnesses' testimonies can only be partially considered due to their weakened condition and diminished ability to remember what they saw during that time. Furthermore, after thirty years, it is possible that they may be fantasizing. Therefore, no definite conclusion can be reached that those shootings actually took place, who did the shooting, and if the accused [Schmidt] took part in such." In addition, the Minister ruled that the statute of limitations for the crime of homicide had run out.

Never arrested or even condemned, Max Schmidt died on April 13, 2001.

Our head kapo, Joseph Hermann, left Neustadt with my brother and me, his name having been changed in the naval hospital, by accident, to Hermann Joseph. He kept this version because it sounded, in his words, "less Jewish." He became Deputy Chairman of the Bavarian Social Democratic Party, then Minister of Renovation for Bavaria. He was the leading candidate for Minister of Educational and Cultural Affairs for Bavaria in 1948 when several former prisoners accused him of murder and American military officers arrested him.

Hermann was tried in Ansbach in July of 1950 on fifty-three charges of abusing prisoners. Over a hundred witnesses testified, fifty-eight of them former inmates. On May 12, 1953, the court acquitted Hermann of all charges. In the court's opinion, no *reliable* witnesses to specific events could be found. Hermann died in December, 1997.

Count Folke Bernadotte is reported to have saved close to thirty thousand concentration camp prisoners. In 1948 the United Nations posted him to the Middle East to negotiate a settlement between the Israelis and the Palestinians. On September 17 Jewish extremists assassinated him in an ambush in Jerusalem.

After the war, Johnny Baldwin flew in Egypt and Iraq, then in Korea, "attached to the USAF's 16th Fighter Interceptor Squadron of the 51st Fighter Interceptor Wing, flying F-86 Sabers [jets]. . . .

"On March 15, 1952, after flying eight sorties on Sabers, he was reported missing from a weather reconnaissance in the Sariwon area. It seems that Baldwin's Saber was not seen again after an attempted cloud break in mountainous country, although there have been unsubstantiated reports that he was accidentally shot down by his wingman." Baldwin is officially recorded as missing in action.

The RAF still considers him "the supreme Typhoon pilot of World War II."

The various Typhoon squadrons were disbanded between August 30 and September 15, 1945. The RAF gathered up all Typhoon aircraft in 1946–1947 and scrapped them. Today, only one Typhoon remains—MN235—at the RAF Museum, Hendon, England. It is not operational.

Fritz Hallerstede remained in Neustadt for many years in his house overlooking the beach. His heroic actions on May 3 are a source of pride to his descendants, as I discovered when I had the good fortune to meet his son in May, 2000.

I never discovered either the name or the whereabouts of the fisherman who saved my life.

After the war I lived in Frankfurt, overseeing some three hundred survivors in a bombed-out hotel. The American headquarters kitchen at the Frankfurt Airport provided us with soup. After a while I joined my brother Josek in Lüdenscheid. In August of 1945, I visited the house of a Mr. Teichmann, who was privately conducting Rosh Hashanah services. There I met his daughter Else, who in time became my wife.

Josek and I eventually emigrated to the United States, traveling on an old U.S. Army troop ship, the SS *Fletcher*. When we arrived in New York Harbor and saw the Statue of Liberty, we wept. Traveling to Boston, we were taken in by a generous great-uncle who made a point of tracking down as many relatives as he could and bringing them to the United States. In 1950 I returned to Germany, married Else, and brought her to the United States. Josek (who used "Joseph" in the United States) and I opened an electronics business together in Boston, Shawmut TV and Appliance Center, which we ran for many years. With his second wife, Helen Richmond, Josek had a son, Victor. My brother died in 1965.

To date no British government has made reference to the deaths of the thousands of people in Neustadt Bay. There has been no official explanation, no request for forgiveness, no proposed memorial.

Richard Clarke—the former U.S. counterterrorism adviser to three presidents—offered an explanation and made a plea for forgiveness in his March 24, 2004, statement to the September 11 Commission in Washington, DC. For this, the families and loved ones of the victims of that tragedy warmly thanked him.

Is it too much to ask the same of a government, over half a century later?

On Poel Island, inhabitants built a memorial to the victims of the disaster, carting stones up from the beach throughout the summer of 1945. "We wanted to show what we thought," explained then-mayor Fritz Reich, who personally helped gather and bury the bodies that washed ashore. The mason who built the memorial said, "This is the least I could do for the unfortunate [people] from the *Cap Arcona.*"

In the small Jewish cemetery in Neustadt, headstones carry just the date of death—May 3, 1945—and the concentration camp numbers of the inmates buried there, the only means by which they could be identified: KZ 56691, KZ 363, KZ 5437, etc. A stele reads, in German and English: ERECTED TO THE MEMORY OF THE MEN AND WOMEN OF THE JEWISH FAITH WHO DIED UNDER THE EVIL OPPRESSION OF NAZI GERMANY. THOSE BURIED IN THIS PLACE DIED ON AND AFTER THE DAY OF LIBERATION, MAY 3, 1945.

In 1971, a twelve-year-old boy from Hamburg found "the complete bones of a young man" washed up on a beach near Neustadt where he and his family were swimming and sunbathing while on vacation. Police took them away in a bucket.

In 1972 I returned to Neustadt with my wife, Else. In nearby Timmendorf, we found two cemeteries overgrown with weeds. Here lie some of the victims. One stone says simply, THOSE BURIED IN THIS PLACE DIED IN NEUSTADT ON MAY 3, 1945. Compared to the crime they memorialize, the cemeteries are very obscure.

Vacationers' campgrounds now stand on the peaceful shores of Neustadt Bay, sheltered by low dunes and occasional stands of poplars. Visitors come to swim and to soak up the sun. The persevering visitor may find the main memorial to the victims of May 3,

1945. It has three plinths, the central one displaying an inverted triangle, the symbol Nazis used to categorize Jews. At first all Jews were required to wear yellow triangles. Smaller memorials are scattered throughout the area.

Those who perished were not just prisoners. They were tough, tenacious, unrelenting fighters, with hearts stubborn enough to survive all the Nazis had cast upon them. And yet, they died on the very doorstep of freedom.

Since the fiftieth anniversary of the incident, May 3, 1995, when a special commemoration was held, the history of the catastrophe has been depicted in the *Cap Arcona* Museum in Neustadt.

To this day, neither the German nor the British government has apologized for the Neustadt Bay tragedy or recognized its victims.

For the last several years, I have gone to Germany each spring to commemorate the victims of the disaster, walking with others from the town of Neustadt to the shore of the bay on one of the several dirt roads named for the concentration camps. My choice is usually "Auschwitz."

Walking up the last hill to the shore, I see, both to the left and the right, the graves of nameless people. One cemetery, fenced in by stones, has the inscription, JEWISH VICTIMS.

As I reach the shore, I am overcome with emotion. Scenes from the *Cap Arcona* sinking and other horrific sights that I have tried to suppress threaten to overwhelm me. By now, all those participating have handkerchiefs in their hands, which they put frequently to their faces.

I stand facing the quiet waves, trying to maintain my civility in the face of the horrific memory. This is where brothers, sisters, fathers, mothers, aunts, uncles, nephews, nieces, and other resilient concentration camp prisoners—who survived years of Nazi cruelty—were sent to the bottom of the sea.

In the week to come, I will be speaking at academic institutions in the area to describe for new generations what the Third Reich did to us and others.

This spring visit is and always will be my debt and duty.

APPENDIX A:

SIGNIFICANT INDIVIDUALS

Prisoners

Myself, Benjamin Jacobs, born Berek Jakubowicz

Joseph Jacobs, born Josek Jakubowicz, my older brother

Willy and Vikky Engel, Czechoslovakian twins, special friends
of ours

Joseph Hermann, head kapo (trusty) of my group of prisoners

Germans

Heinrich Himmler, Reichsführer (Empire Leader)-SS,
Head of Gestapo and Interior Minister,
with chief responsibility for concentration camps

Walter Schellenberg, Brigadeführer (Brigadier General)-SS,
influential aide of Himmler

Karl Kaufmann, Obergruppenführer (Lieutenant General)-SS,
Gauleiter (Territorial Commander) of Schleswig-Holstein

Ernst Kaltenbrunner, Obergruppenführer (Lieutenant
    General)-SS, Chief of SS Intelligence,
    Chief of Reich Security

Max Pauly, Sturmbannführer (Major)-SS, Commandant of
    Neuengamme concentration camp

Max Schmidt, Scharführer (Sergeant)-SS,
    commandant of my group of prisoners

Heinrich Bertram, Captain, *Cap Arcona*

Johann Jacobsen, Captain, *Thielbek*

Carl Steincke, Captain, *Deutschland*

Fritz Nobmann, Captain, *Athen*

Fritz Hallerstede, Neustadt resident and boatman

Americans

Dwight D. Eisenhower, General, Supreme Commander,
    Allied Expeditionary Forces

Omar N. Bradley, General, Commander, U.S. 12th Army Group

George S. Patton, Lieutenant General,
    Commander, U.S. 3rd Army

William H. Simpson, Lieutenant General,
    Commander, U.S. 9th Army

British

Bernard Law Montgomery, Field Marshal, Commander,
    21st Army Group

Miles G. Dempsey, Lieutenant General, Commander, 2nd Army

G. P. B. "Pip" Roberts, Major General,
    Commander, 11th Armored Division

C. M. Barber, Major General, 15th (Scottish)
     Infantry Division

Derek Mills-Roberts, Brigadier General,
     Commander, 1st Commando Brigade

Sir John B. Churcher, Major General, Commander,
     159th Infantry Brigade

Sir Arthur "Bomber" Harris, Air Chief Marshal,
     Royal Air Force Bomber Command

Sir Arthur Coningham, Air Marshal, 2nd Tactical Air Force

Derek Stevenson, Squadron Leader,
     No. 184 Typhoon Squadron, RAF

Johnny Baldwin, Squadron Leader, No. 198
     Typhoon Squadron, RAF

Martin Rumbold, Squadron Leader,
     No. 263 Typhoon Squadron, RAF

L. W. F. "Pinkie" Stark, Squadron Leader,
     No. 609 Typhoon Squadron, RAF

Swedish

Folke Bernadotte, Count, Vice-Chairman, Swedish Red Cross

Swiss

P. de Blonay, Head, International Red Cross, Lübeck

Russians

Georgi K. Zhukov, Marshal, Deputy Commander
     in Chief, Soviet Armies

Appendix B:

Significant Military Units (All British)

Ground Forces

21st Army Group (Field Marshal Bernard
 Law Montgomery, Commanding)

2nd Army (Lieutenant General Miles Dempsey)

11th Armored Division (Major General G. P. B. "Pip" Roberts)

15th (Scottish) Infantry Division (Major General C. M. Barber),
 Inns of Court Regiment

1st Special Services (later, 1st Commando) Brigade (Brigadier
 General Derek Mills-Roberts)

3, 6 (Army) Commando

45, 46 Royal Marine Commando

159th Infantry Brigade (Major General John B. Churcher)

30th Assault Unit

AIR FORCES

Royal Air Force Bomber Command

(Air Chief Marshal Arthur "Bomber" Harris)

2nd Tactical Air Force

(Air Marshal Sir Arthur Coningham)

No. 2 Group

No. 83 Group

No. 84 Group

Royal Air Force Typhoon Squadrons

No. 184 (Squadron Leader Derek Stevenson)

No. 193 (D. M. Taylor)

No. 197 (K. J. Harding)

No. 198 (Johnny Baldwin)

No. 263 (Martin Rumbold)

No. 609 (L. W. F. "Pinkie" Stark)

Appendix C:

SS Ranks and British/USA Equivalents

Oberstgruppenführer	General
Obergruppenführer	Lieutenant General
Gruppenführer	Major General
Brigadeführer	Brigadier General
Standartenführer	Colonel
Obersturmbannführer	Lieutenant Colonel
Sturmbannführer	Major
Hauptsturmführer	Captain
Obersturmführer	1st Lieutenant
Untersturmführer	2nd Lieutenant
Sturmscharführer	Master Sergeant
Hauptscharführer	Technical Sergeant
Oberscharführer	Staff Sergeant
Scharführer	Sergeant
Unterscharführer	Corporal
Rottenführer	Private First Class
Sturmann	Private

APPENDIX D:

SOURCES

Ambrose, Stephen. *Eisenhower, Volume I: Soldier, General of the Army, President-Elect, 1890–1952*. New York: Simon & Schuster, 1983.

Armitage, Michael. *The Royal Air Force*. London: Cassell & Co., 1993.

Barker, Ralph. *The RAF at War*. New York: Time-Life Books, 1981.

Berben, Paul. *Dachau, 1933–1945: The Official History*. London: Norfolk Press, 1975.

Bernadotte, Folke. *Instead of Arms*. London: Hodder and Stoughton, 1949.

———. *The Curtain Falls: Last Days of the Third Reich*. New York: Alfred A. Knopf, 1945.

Bertram, Heinrich. "Report to the Hamburg-Südamerika Line, January 31, 1947," as reported in Volfer, Joachim. *Biographie eines Schiffes*. Herfort: Koehlers Verlagsgesellschaft, 1949.

Blair, Clay. *Hitler's U-Boat War*. New York: Random House, 1998.

Bond, Lawrence. *Typhoons' Last Storm*, The History Channel film, 2000.

Churchill, Winston. *The Second World War: Volume 6: Triumph and Tragedy*. Boston: Houghton Mifflin, 1953.

————. *The Second World War: Volume 7: Road to Victory*. Boston: Houghton Mifflin, 1986.

Delaforce, Patrick. *The Black Bull: From Normandy to the Baltic with the 11th Armored Division*. Phoenix Mill: Sutton Publishing, 1993.

de Zayas, Alfred. *The Wehrmacht War Crimes Bureau, 1939–1945*, the University of Nebraska Press, 1989.

Dickens, A. G. *Lübeck Diary*. London: Gollancz, 1947.

Eisenhower, Dwight D. *Crusade in Europe*. New York: Doubleday & Co., 1948.

Fleming, Gerald. *Hitler and the Final Solution*. Berkeley: University of California Press, 1984.

Franks, Norman. *Typhoon Attack*. London: William Kimber, 1984.

Giblin, James Cross. *The Life and Death of Adolf Hitler*. New York: Clarion Books, 2002.

Gilbert, Martin. *The Day the War Ended: May 8, 1945: Victory in Europe*. New York: Henry Holt & Co., 1995.

————. *The Holocaust: A History of the Jews in Europe During World War II*. New York: Holt, Rinehart & Winston, 1986.

———. *Winston S. Churchill: Road to Victory 1941-1945, Vol. VII*. Boston: Houghton Mifflin Co., 1986.

Goguel, Rudi. *Cap Arcona*. Frankfurt am Main: Röderburg, 1972.

Hansen, Reimer. "Victory and 'Zero Hour' 1945" in *History Today*, May, 1995.

Hastings, Max. *Bomber Command: The Myths and Realities of the Strategic Bombing Offensive, 1939–1945*. New York: Dial Press, 1979.

Hermann, Karl and Günter Klaucke. *Der Fall* Cap Arcona, 1995.

Horne, Alistair with David Montgomery. *Monty, the Lonely Leader, 1944–1945*. New York: Harpercollins, 1994.

Jacobs, Benjamin. *The Dentist of Auschwitz: A Memoir*. Louisville: University Press of Kentucky, 1995.

Jefford, C. G. *RAF Squadrons: A Comprehensive Record Since 1912*. Shrewsbury: Airlife Publishing, 1988.

Johnson, Group Capt. J. E. "Fighting Talk: Tactics of Aerial Warfare" in Sunderman, James F. (ed.), *World War II in the Air*. New York: Franklin Watts, 1948.

Keegan, John, ed. *The Collins Atlas of the Second World War*. Ann Arbor: Border Press, 2003.

Lange, Wilhelm. Cap Arcona *Dokumentation*. Struve: Eutin, 1988.

Leckie, Robert. *Delivered from Evil: The Saga of World War II*. New York: Harper & Row, 1987.

Levin, Nora. *The Holocaust: The Destruction of European Jewry, 1933–1945*. New York: Thomas Y. Crowell, 1968.

Liddell-Hart, B. H. *The Tanks: The History of the Royal Tank Regiment, Vol. II*. New York: Praeger, 1959.

Mills-Roberts, Derek. *Clash by Night: A Commando Chronicle*. London: William Kimber, 1956.

Montgomery, Bernard. *El Alamein to the River Sangro: Normandy to the Baltic*. London: Hutchinson & Co., 1947.

Nesbit, Roy C. *Coastal Command in Action 1939–1945*. Phoenix Mill: Budding Books, 2000.

———. *Failed to Return: Mysteries of the Air 1939–1945*. Bath: Patrick Stephens, 1988.

Nesbit, William. "The *Cap Arcona* Disaster," *Aeroplane Monthly*, June, 1984.

Nutting, David and Jim Glanville. *Attain by Surprise: The Story of 30 Assault Unit Royal Navy/Royal Marine Commando and of Intelligence by Capture*. Chichester: David Colver, 1997.

Padfield, Peter. *Dönitz, the Last Führer: Portrait of a Nazi War Leader*. New York: Harper & Row, 1984.

———. *Himmler: Reichsführer-SS*. New York: Henry Holt & Co., 1990.

Persico, Joseph E. *Roosevelt's Secret War: FDR and World War II Espionage*. New York: Random House, 2001.

Richards, Denis and Hilary Saunders. *The Royal Air Force 1939–1945*. London: Her Majesty's Stationery Office, 1954.

Samain, Bryan. *Commando Men: The Story of a Royal Commando in North West Europe*. London: Stevens & Son, 1948.

Schön, Heinz. *Die* Cap Arcona *Katastrophe*. Stuttgart: Motor Buch Verlag, 1989.

Schwarberg, Günter. *Angriffsziel* Cap Arcona. Göttingen: Steidi, 1998.

Sims, Edward H. *The Greatest Aces*. New York: Harper & Row, 1967.

The RAF in the Bombing Offensive Against Germany, Vol. 6, 1945, AIR 41/56.

Thomas, Chris. *Typhoon and Tempest Aces of World War 2*. Botley: Osprey Publishing, 1999.

Thompson, R. W. *Winston Churchill: The Yankee Marlborough*. New York: Doubleday and Co., 1963.

Toland, John. *The Last 100 Days*. New York: Random House, 1965.

Valent, Dani. "Curator of Nightmares," *The Age*, January 26, 2002.

Von Krockow, Christian. *Hour of the Women*. New York: Harper Collins, 1991.

Whitaker, Denis and Shelagh Whitaker. *Rhineland: The Battle to End the War*. New York: St. Martin's Press, 1989.

NOTES

PROLOGUE

No One Tells This Story

"one of the . . . known." Lawrence Bond, *Typhoons' Last Storm.*

CHAPTER ONE

No Prisoner Is to Fall into Enemy Hands Alive

"The fuel production . . . economic collapse." Albert Speer, June 20, 1946, Nuremberg Trials, *The Nizkor Project*, page 30.

"in the north . . . French Army." Ted Ballard, U.S. Army Center of Military History, "Rhineland, 15 September 1944–21 March 1945," at www.army.mil/cmhpg/brochures/rhineland/rhineland.htm

"so that . . . Swiss border." Ibid.

"The airborne attack . . . North German plain." Charles B. MacDonald, *The Siegfried Line Campaign*, pages 429–430, at www.army.mil/cmh-pg/books/70-7_19.htm

"The biggest . . . happened." www.ramskov.nu

"The operation . . . somewhat singular." Charles B. MacDonald, *The Siegfried Line Campaign*, page 442.

"The moment . . . set down." Winston Churchill, *The Second World War: Volume 6: Triumph and Tragedy*, page 227.

"The great . . . good." Stephen Ambrose, *Eisenhower*, page 353.

"an all-out offensive . . . of 1945." Ted Ballard, U.S. Army Center of Military History, "Rhineland."

"Montgomery . . . personally." Max Hastings, *Bomber Command*, page 339.

"by 1944 . . . economic drain." Ted Ballard, U.S. Army Center of Military History, "Rhineland."

"Why should we . . . the Russians?" Timothy Naftali, "The Hardest Job on the Longest Day," *The New York Times*, July 28, 2002.

"Unless . . . in defense." Stephen Ambrose, *Eisenhower*, page 382.

"There were . . . the Pacific." Forrest C. Pogue, "The Decision to Halt at the Elbe," at http://www.army.mil/cmh-pg/books/70-7_22.htm

"that the only way . . . destroy it." Stephen Ambrose, *Eisenhower*, page 357.

CHAPTER TWO

Where Could They Be Taking Us?

"[As early as] . . . the camps." Joseph E. Persico, *Roosevelt's Secret War*, page 219.

"Solid intelligence . . . 30,000?" Ibid.

"Curiously . . . the situation." Ibid.

"For some time . . . witnesses." Count Folke Bernadotte, *The Curtain Falls*, page 17.

"ordered a tank . . . its name." Major Scott T. Glass, *Quartermaster Professional Bulletin*, Autumn, 1997.

"a daring . . . failure." John Keegan (ed.), *The Collins Atlas of the Second World War*, page 160.

"Children were shot. . . target practice." George Duncan, "Massacres and Atrocities of World War II," www.inet.net.au/rgduncan

"Many, indeed . . . the pigs." Christian von Krockow, *Hour of the Women*, pages 83–84.

On one day . . . 11,000 sorties. Ralph Barker, *The RAF at War*, page 161.

"the progressive . . . weakened." Max Hastings, *Bomber Command*, page 344.

"The zones . . . the meeting." Forrest C. Pogue, "The Decision to Halt at the Elbe."

"I didn't say . . . could do." Robert Dallek, *Franklin Roosevelt and American Foreign Policy*, at http://history.acusd.edu/gen/20th/coldwar1.html

CHAPTER THREE

Special Instructions in Case of War

"For those of us . . . household knowledge." Hon. James E. Baker, personal communication, September 9, 2003.

"the epic theme . . . be bettered." Titanic Historical Society, http://home.earthlink.net/~wwwalden/Titanic-1943/SelpinArticle.htm

"a decoration . . . seduced." David Stuart Hull, *Film and the Third Reich*, excerpt at The Titanic Historical Society, http://home.earthlink.net/~wwwalden/Titanic-1943/SelpinArticle.htm

"Sometime . . . to death." Ibid.

"American airmen . . . alternative." Max Hastings, *Bomber Command*, page 339.

"Bombing . . . nothing." Ibid., page 337.

"Night after . . . the cities." Ibid.

"It is difficult . . . and alert." Torsten Brandel, *Svenska Dagbladet*, April 23, 1975, at www.sweden.se/templates/FactSheet___4198.asp

"ostensibly . . . camps." Peter Padfield, *Himmler: Reichsführer-SS*, page 565.

"I suddenly saw . . . heavy." Folke Bernadotte, *The Curtain Falls*, page 42.

"[Musy] had come . . . this kind." Ibid., page 47.

"be released . . . Sweden." Ibid., pages 50–51.

"I told . . . unthinkable." Ibid., page 51.

"the Norwegians . . . Swedes." Ibid., page 52.

"somewhere . . . three thousand." Folke Bernadotte, *The Curtain Falls*, page 52.

"promised . . . later." Ibid., page 61.

"On March 7 . . . the West." Denis Whitaker and Shelagh Whitaker, *Rhineland: The Battle to End the War*, page 266.

"Remagen . . . needed." Ibid.

"to destroy . . . enemy hands." Peter Padfield, *Himmler: Reichsführer-SS*, page 567.

"all organized . . . had ceased." Patrick Delaforce, *The Black Bull*, page 231.

"if the program . . . would vanish." Folke Bernadotte, *The Curtain Falls*, page 65.

"instructing . . . rolling stock." Peter Padfield, *Himmler: Reichsführer-SS*, page 57.

"Without benefit . . . yesterday." R. W. Thompson, *Winston Churchill: The Yankee Marlborough*, pages 324–325.

"the slim ribbon . . . targets." Bryan Samain, *Commando Men*, page 141.

"The same flag . . . World War II." B. H. Liddell-Hart, *The Tanks, Vol. II*, page 434.

"In all . . . the Rhine." Ibid., page 436.

"The River . . . 'V' weapon." Derek Mills-Roberts, *Clash by Night*, page 143.

Chapter Four

The Queen of the South Atlantic

"Prisoners . . . Neustadt." Anonymous, *The Suffering of 400 Concentration-Camp Prisoners on Their March from Blankenburg/Harz to Schleswig-Holstein, and the Shipwreck of the* Cap Arcona, WO 309/1788, page 3.

"Out of the waves . . . New Worlds." Heinz Schön, *Die* Cap Arcona *Katastrophe*, page 26.

"[T]he capture . . . airfields." Denis Richards and Hilary Saunders, *The Royal Air Force 1939–1945*, page 288.

"the first . . . World War Two." http://www.raf.mod.uk/history/h184.html

"a number of Jews." Folke Bernadotte, *The Curtain Falls*, page 83.

"It seems . . . impressive." Winston Churchill, Memo to his Chiefs of Staff Committee, March 28, 1945.

"It is impossible . . . bombing." Max Hastings, *Bomber Command*, page 344.

"the Baltic . . . resistance." www.rickard.karoo.net

"The accusation . . . grenadier." Max Hastings, *Bomber Command*, page 344.

"I thought . . . human beings there . . . ." Folke Bernadotte, *The Curtain Falls*, page 85.

"all Danish . . . the sick." Peter Padfield, *Himmler: Reichsführer-SS*, page 578.

"the dispatch. . . French citizens." Ibid., page 89.

"capitulation . . . front." Ibid., page 578.

"that Hitler . . . with Neuengamme." Ibid.,page 94.

"the long lines . . . gave out." Ibid., page 70.

"German fighter planes . . . interference." Ibid., page 71.

"German troops . . . was the end." Ibid., page 75.

"the RAF . . . at bay." Patrick Delaforce, *The Black Bull*, page 239.

"Storch . . . countermanded." Gerald Fleming, *Hitler and the Final Solution*, page 176.

"Max Schmidt . . . occurrence." Anonymous, *The Suffering of 400 Concentration-Camp Prisoners*, page 1.

CHAPTER FIVE

A Special Operation

"On the . . . carried on." Maj. Noel Till, *Report on Investigations*, WO 309/1592, page 10.

"fanning out . . . the Elbe." Bryan Samain, *Commando Men*, page 169.

"on this voyage . . . architect." Anonymous, *The Suffering of 400 Concentration-Camp Prisoners*, page 2.

"on this march . . . twice a week." Ibid.

"[instructed] . . . immediately." Peter Padfield, *Himmler*, page 582.

"Handing-over . . . alive.' " Paul Berben, *Dachau*, page 184.

"by inference . . . Neuengamme." Roy C. Nesbit, *Failed to Return*, page 170.

"[I]n the middle . . . 'Cloud A-1.' " Nizkor Project, "Nuremberg Trials: Kaltenbrunner," April 11, 1946, page 275.

"For the . . . poison." Ibid.

"formally . . . bombing." Max Hastings, *Bomber Command*, page 344.

"Winston . . . northwards." Struan Robertson, www.rrz.uni-hamburg. de/rz3a035/arcona.html

"Today . . . camps." www.sweden.se/templates/FactSheet__4No. 198.asp

"For me . . . such masses." Benjamin Jacobs, *The Dentist of Auschwitz*, page 192.

"The reason . . . lies." Folke Bernadotte, *The Curtain Falls*, page 99.

"The very next . . . lying." Ibid.

CHAPTER SIX

This Insane Order

"We . . . unbelievable." Philip Jackson, WO 309/1592, page 4.

"About . . . slopped about." Karl Hermann and Günter Klaucke, *Der Fall Cap Arcona*.

"swing . . . light." Lawrence Bond, *Typhoons' Last Storm*.

"There were . . . above us." Mikelis Mezmalietis, Report, page 3.

"[gave] . . . handed in." Noel Till, *Report on Investigations*, WO 309/1592, page 11

"throw . . . the ship." Ibid.

"allowed . . . nationalities." Folke Bernadotte, *The Curtain Falls*, page 102.

"2,873 . . . Ravensbrück." www.sweden.se/templates/FactSheet__4No. 198.asp

"he had . . . troops." Gerald Fleming, *Hitler and the Final Solution*, pages 179–180.

"Himmler . . . Norway." Folke Bernadotte, *The Curtain Falls*, pages 112–113.

"The dead . . . sardines." Johann Jacobsen letter, collection of
Benjamin Jacobs.

"at 4:40 . . . superiors." Martin Gilbert, *Winston S. Churchill: Road to
Victory, 1941-1945*, page 1312.

"Gehrig . . . ship." Benjamin Jacobs, *The Dentist of Auschwitz*, page 193.

"I have . . . order." Karl Hermann and Günter Klaucke,
Der Fall Cap Arcona.

"Gehrig . . . board." Benjamin Jacobs, *The Dentist of Auschwitz*,
page 192.

According to . . . lifeboats. Struan Robertson, www.rrz.uni-hamburg.de/
rz3a035/arcona.html

"[T]he rumor . . . that way." Karl Hermann and Günter Klaucke,
Der Fall Cap Arcona.

"Some of . . . their fears." Roy C. Nesbit, *Failed to Return*, page 170.

"It is probable . . . the last." Ibid.

"[When] . . . prisoners." Karl Hermann and Günter Klaucke,
Der Fall Cap Arcona.

"Relations . . . the SS." William Nesbit, "The *Cap Arcona* Disaster,"
Aeroplane Monthly, June 1984, page 289.

"No attempt . . . refused." Roy C. Nesbit, *Failed to Return*, page 171.

" 'A German offer . . . United States.' " Folke Bernadotte, *The Curtain
Falls*, page 116.

"divisional . . . Torgau." Martin Gilbert, *Winston S. Churchill: Road to
Victory, 1941-1945*, page 1312.

"In a . . . Kiel." Clay Blair, *Hitler's U-Boat War*, page 699.

"There is no . . . restored." Martin Gilbert, *Winston S. Churchill: Road to
Victory, 1941-1945*, page 1302.

"The war . . . Schleswig-Holstein." Bryan Samain, *Commando Men*,
pages 179–180.

"to request . . . Neustadt." Benjamin Jacobs, *The Dentist
of Auschwitz*, page 193.

"moving east . . . troops." Bryan Samain, *Commando Men*, page 182.

"the Athen . . . on board:" Noel Till, *Report on Investigations*, WO 309/1592, page 11.

"urged . . . the war.' " Folke Bernadotte, *The Curtain Falls*, page 124.

"were not . . . position." Ibid., page 154.

CHAPTER SEVEN

I Saw So Many Dead

"on May 1st . . . handful." Mikelis Mezmalietis, Report, page 4.

"On the ground . . . April." *The RAF in the Bombing Offensive Against Germany*, Vol. 6, 45, AIR 41/56, page 243.

"Air attacks . . . time." Operations Record Book, 2nd TAF, May 1, 1945, page 44.

"After...night." Ibid., pages 44–45.

"At the beginning . . . transport." HQ No. 83 Group, May, 1945, AIR 25/698, page 1.

"Traffic . . . profusion." Ibid.

"only . . . British." John Toland, *The Last 100 Days*, pages 552–553.

"[I]t could now . . . forces." Bernard Montgomery, *El Alamein to the River Sangro*, page 399.

"ships . . . strike." AIR 41/68, page 243.

"sail[ing] . . . appalling." Philip Jackson, WO 309/1592, page 5.

"With . . . tugs." Noel Till, *Report on Investigations*, WO 309/1592, page 12.

"They . . . Lübeck." Patrick Delaforce, *The Black Bull*, page 273.

"[It] appear[ed] . . . Travemünde."Arthur Dickens, *Lübeck Diary*, page 134.

"on 2nd May . . . authority." Noel Till, *Report on Investigations*, WO 309/1592, page 13.

"A postwar . . . afire." Ibid., page 18.

"The prisoners . . . they did." Karl Hermann and Günter Klaucke, *Der Fall* Cap Arcona.

"the crew . . . to shore." Dani Valent, "Curator of Nightmares," *The Age*, January 26, 2002.

"the sick . . . like that." Martin Gilbert, *The Day the War Ended*, page 71.

"news of . . . barges." Anonymous, "Notes on the Shooting of Stutthof KZ prisoners at Neustadt," WO 309/851.

" 'finding . . . to shore.' " Gail Hollenbeck, *St. Petersburg Times*, April 20, 2002.

"With the first . . . turned red." Dani Valent, "Curator of Nightmares," *The Age*, January 26, 2002.

"At short range . . . marines." Christopher Report, WO 309/851.

"The police . . . were kept." Noel Till, *Report on Investigations*, WO 309/1592, page 20.

"along . . . or more." Günther Schwarberg, *Angriffsziel* Cap Arcona, pages 72–73.

"I myself . . . school." Fritz Hallerstede statement, October 17, 1952, page 2.

CHAPTER EIGHT

A Flying Wrecking Ball

"A considerable amount . . . the Baltic." Summary of Events, 2nd Tactical Air Force, May 2, 1945, AIR 24/1498, page 2.

"[I]t was believed . . . that country." Michael Armitage, *The Royal Air Force*, page 149.

"The intelligence . . . with them." Lawrence Bond, *Typhoons' Last Storm*.

"although . . . weapon." Roy C. Nesbit, *Coastal Command in Action 1939–1945*, page 149.

"spotted . . . anger." www.609.org.uk

"a technical nightmare." Chris Thomas, *Typhoon and Tempest Aces of World War 2*, page 22.

"In the first . . . assemblies." http://www.military.cz/british/air/war/fighter/tempest/history.htm

"the aircraft . . . wrecking ball." Alex Rogers, "Hawker Typhoon 1B."

"They were . . . messing around . . ." Norman Franks, *Typhoon Attack*, page 16.

"to ensure . . . Eastern Front." Reimer Hansen, "Victory and 'Zero Hour' 1945" in *History Today*, May 1995.

"large-scale . . . safe action." 83 Group Operation Order No. 71, May 3, 1945, AIR 24/1518.

"the large . . . fleet of war." Summary of Events, 2nd Tactical Air Force, May 3, 1945, AIR 24/1498.

"Main interest . . . Kiel . . ." Ibid.

"We had . . . fight." Günther Schwarberg, *Angriffsziel* Cap Arcona, page 13.

"Hospital . . . attacked." 83 Group Operation Order 72, May 3, 1945, AIR 25/698.

"Nos. 83 . . . (27,561 tons)." *The RAF in the Bombing Offensive Against Germany, Vol. 6*, AIR 41/56.

"We flew . . . submarines." Lawrence Bond, *Typhoons' Last Storm*.

"He had . . . coast." Peter Padfield, *Dönitz, The Last Führer*, page 420.

"A major! . . . headquarters?" Alistair Horne with David Montgomery, *Monty, the Lonely Leader, 1944–1945*, page 505.

"With Rumbold . . . Coles." These names and pilots' names in squadrons on subsequent pages, Wilhelm Lange, Cap Arcona *Dockumentation*, pages 81–92.

"Going . . . down!" Lawrence Bond, *Typhoons' Last Storm*.

"You roll . . . [target]." Edward Sims, *The Greatest Aces*, page 199.

"You're . . . lose it." Lawrence Bond, *Typhoons' Last Storm*.

CHAPTER NINE

God Help Us!

"a meteoric . . . experience." Chris Thomas, *Typhoon and Tempest Aces of World War 2*, page 75.

"managing . . . minutes." Ibid, page 77.

"[P. W.] . . . back." AIR 27/1170, page 1.

"F/Sgt . . . Base." Ibid.

"forced-landed . . . leak." Ibid.

"the . . . shot up." Günther Schwarberg, *Angriffsziel* Cap Arcona, page 86.

"There were hundreds . . . overboard." Philip Jackson, WO 309/1592, page 5.

"The after . . . grab." Günther Schwarberg, *Angriffsziel*
Cap Arcona, page 87.

"Eight . . . Bay." No. 263 Operations Records Book, May 3, 1945, AIR 27/1548, page 1.

"A 10,000 . . . stern." Ibid.

"At the . . . capsize.' " Günther Schwarberg, *Angriffsziel* Cap Arcona, page 87.

CHAPTER TEN

How Could We Part?

"At the stairs . . . him." Günther Schwarberg, *Angriffsziel* Cap Arcona, page 98.

"One . . . float." Ibid.

"the water . . . fried:" Karl Hermann and Günter Klaucke,
Der Fall Cap Arcona.

CHAPTER ELEVEN

I Will Not Let Go

"The Germans . . . soundless[ly]." Günther Schwarberg, *Angriffsziel* Cap Arcona, page 102.

"Being . . . ships." Philip Jackson, WO 309/1592, page 5.

"during the attack . . . rescued." Günther Schwarberg, *Angriffsziel* Cap Arcona, page 102.

"Three . . . rescue." Single Page. No Start or Finish, War Crimes Witnesses papers, WO 309/1592.

"The attack . . . hull." No. 197 Operations Records Book, May 3, 1945, AIR 27/1109, page 1.

"On reaching . . . smoking." Ibid., page 3.

"F/O . . . day." Ibid.

"Time up . . . Neustadt." Operations Record Book. No. 193 Squadron, May 3, 1945.

"In what . . . today." Intelligence Summary No. 266, 2nd Tactical Air Force, May 3, 1945, AIR 24/1498, page 53.

"[W]e could . . . by drowning." Fritz Hallerstede statement, October 17, 1952, page 2.

"never . . . her." Notes on Dina Huberman, Collection of Benjamin Jacobs,

"I saw . . . dangerous." Notes on Möller Investigation, Lübeck, Collection of Benjamin Jacobs.

"The members . . . school." Ibid.

Chapter Twelve

It Didn't Take Very Long

"We had . . . going." Lawrence Bond, *Typhoons' Last Storm*.

"I saw . . . water." Ibid.

"violations . . . necessity." Charter of the International Military Tribunal of Nuremberg, August 8, 1945, The Avalon Project at Yale Law School.

"rights . . . ill-treatment." Hague Ten Convention, October 18, 1907, Article 16, The Avalon Project at Yale Law School.

"the killing . . . principles." Claud Mullins, "The Leipzig Trials," unpaginated excerpt from London: H. F. & G. Whitherby, 1921, at www.gwpda.org/naval/lcastl12.htm

"In particular . . . board." Treaty for the Limitation and Reduction of Armaments, April 22, 1930, Part IV, Article 22.

"September 17, 1942 . . . children." Peter Padfield, *Dönitz, The Last Führer*, page 255.

"waging . . . the Protocol." The Nizkor Project, Nuremberg Transcripts, Judgment: The Defendants: Dönitz, pages 108–109.

"While . . . rafts." Alfred de Zayas, *The Wehrmacht War Crimes Bureau, 1939-1945*, pp. 248-49

"in general . . . task." *The Nizkor Project*, Nuremberg Transcripts, Judgment: The Defendants: Dönitz, page 16.

"encountered . . . freighter." http://www.history.navy.mil/photos/sh-usn/usnsh-w/ss238-k.htm

"It was . . . come." Brad Manera, Australian War Memorial, March 3, 2003.

"We used . . . with me." Lawrence Bond, *Typhoons' Last Storm*.

"Today . . . attacked." No. 198 Operations Record Book, May 3, 1945, AIR 27/1170, page 1.

"I attacked . . . attack them." No. 609 Operations Record Book, May 3, 1945, page 3.

"It . . . thing." Lawrence Bond, *Typhoons' Last Storm*.

"It . . . long." Ibid.

"the chain . . . side." Günther Schwarberg, *Angriffsziel* Cap Arcona, page 106.

"All those . . . weeks." Mikelis Mezmalietis, Report, page 5.

"The 30th . . . to them." David Nutting and Jim Glanville, *Attain by Surprise*, page 225.

"by late . . . gleaned." Ibid., pages 198–199.

"A ship . . . executed." Col. H. G. Sheen Report, June 2, 1945, WO 309/501.

Chapter Thirteen

They Are Surely No Nazis

"When . . . guards." Günther Schwarberg, *Angriffsziel* Cap Arcona, page 117.

"When . . . situation." Derek Mills-Roberts, *Clash by Night*, page 203.

"On May 3 . . . ignorance." Bryan Samain, *Commando Men*, page 187.

"By the . . . them." Derek Mills-Roberts, *Clash by Night*, page 204.

"Large . . . disease." Christopher Report, May 14, 1945,
WO 309/851, page 1

"troops . . . a man." Arthur Dickens, *Lübeck Diary*, pages 133–134.

"on arrival . . . happening." Commanding Officer (CO) 5th Reconnaissance (Recce) Regiment Report, WC/B/16 No. 2 WCIT.

"[We saw] . . . taken." Günther Schwarberg, *Angriffsziel* Cap Arcona,
page 123.

"We found . . . assistance." CO 5 Recce Regiment,
WC/B/16 No. 2 WCIT.

CHAPTER FOURTEEN

Free of Swastikas

"At first light . . . appalling." CO 5 Recce Regiment, WC/B/16 No. 2
WCIT.

"When I . . . range." Christopher Report, WO 309/851.

"We found . . . burial." CO 5 Recce Regimen, WC/B/16 No. 2 WCIT.

"We had . . . German." F. G. Parson, Letter to the *Daily Telegraph*,
March 18, 1982.

"The attitude . . . circumstances." CO 5 Recce Regiment,
WC/B/16 No. 2 WCIT.

EPILOGUE

Where the Living Meet the Dead

"On April 9 . . . killed." Karl Hermann and Günter Klaucke,
Der Fall Cap Arcona.

"It would . . . importance." Wilhelm Lange, Cap Arcona *Dokumentation*,
page 107.

"Personally . . . left." Single Page, No Start or Finish, War Crimes
Witnesses papers, WO 309/1592.

"The story . . . attack." Maj. Stewart Report, WO 309/501.

"in the late afternoon. . . 3,000 tons." Operations Record Book, 2nd TAF,
Apr-May, 1945, AIR 24/1498, page 47.

"commenced . . . murder." Noel Till, *Report on Investigations*, WO 309/1592, pages 5, 16.

"a much depleted . . . warrants." Ibid., page 5.

"the camp . . . the camp." Ibid., page 8.

"On 2nd May . . . authority." Ibid., page 13.

"From the facts . . . ships." Ibid., page 15.

"The Intelligence . . . Investigative Officer." Noel Till, *Report on Investigations*, WO 309/1592, page 14.

"Whatever . . . RAF." Ibid., page 16,

"increased . . . hit." Operations Record Book, 2nd TAF, May 1, 1945, page 44.

"At about 0830 . . . shipping." Operations Record Book, 2nd TAF, Apr-May, 1945, AIR 24/1498, p. 1.

"panic . . . the ships." Denis Richards and Hilary Saunders, *The Royal Air Force 1939–1945*, page 292

"the circumstances . . . relevant." L. E. M. Smith letter, March 20, 1946, FO 371/56890.

"From all . . . damaged." P. J. Coles Letter, April 23, 1946, FO 371/56890.

"refuses . . . later." Lawrence Bond, "British Error Killed WW2 Camp Inmates," *Shanghai Star*, March 7, 2000

"The vast majority . . .100 years." http://www.nationalarchives.gov.uk, March 31, 2004.

"some . . . film." Lawrence Bond, "British Error Killed WW2 Camp Inmates," *Shanghai Star*, March 7, 2000.

"from . . . there." Noel Till, *Report on Investigations*, WO 309/1592, page 22.

"We . . . happened." Karl Hermann and Günter Klaucke, *Der Fall* Cap Arcona.

"We . . . Bay." Max McLeod, "Germany Calling," *Diver*, July 1998.

"Walls . . . silence." *Die Welt*, February 8, 1950.

"jerked . . . teeth." Peter Padfield, *Himmler*, page 611.

"attached . . . wingman." Chris Thomas, *Typhoon and Tempest Aces of World War 2*, page 80.

"the witnesses' . . . in such." Report of Minister of Justice, Schleswig-Holstein, April 19, 1979.

"the supreme . . . World War II." 609 (West Riding) Squadron RAuxAF Newsletter No. 29.

"the complete . . . young man." Günther Schwarberg, *Angriffsziel* Cap Arcona,
page 178.

INDEX

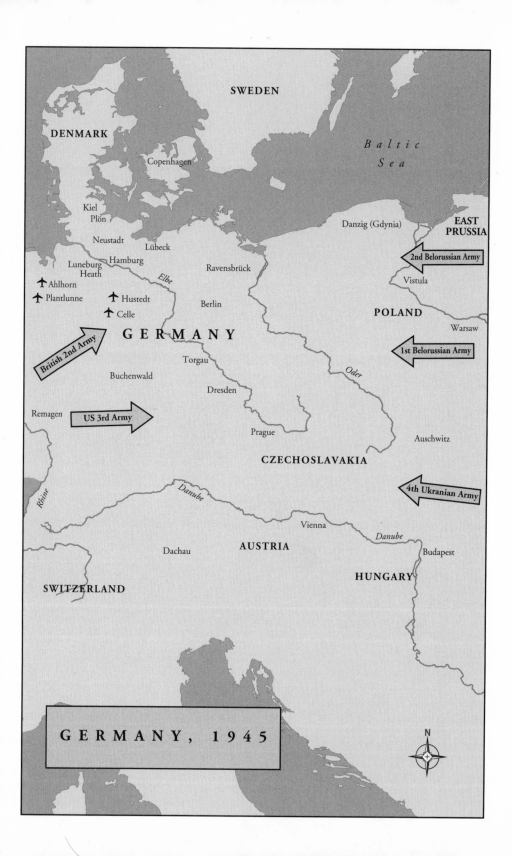

SWEDEN

DENMARK

Copenhagen

Baltic Sea

Kiel
Plön

Danzig (Gdynia)

EAST PRUSSIA

Neustadt
Lübeck

Hamburg

Ravensbrück

Vistula

Luneburg
Heath

Elbe

⚔ Ahlhorn

⚔ Plantlunne   ⚔ Hustedt
              ⚔ Celle

GERMANY

Berlin

POLAND

Warsaw

◁ 2nd Belorussian Army

◁ 1st Belorussian Army

British 2nd Army ▷

Torgau

Oder

Buchenwald

Remagen   US 3rd Army ▷

Dresden

Prague

Auschwitz

CZECHOSLAVAKIA

4th Ukranian Army ◁

Danube

Rhine

Vienna

Danube

Budapest

Dachau

AUSTRIA

SWITZERLAND

HUNGARY

G E R M A N Y ,   1 9 4 5

N